D1603544

MEMOIRES

for Paul de Man

Jacques Derrida

MEMOIRES
for Paul de Man

*The Wellek Library Lectures
at the University of California, Irvine*

Translated by Cecile Lindsay, Jonathan Culler,
and Eduardo Cadava

COLUMBIA UNIVERSITY PRESS   NEW YORK 1986

Translations edited by Avital Ronell and Eduardo Cadava

Library of Congress Cataloging-in-Publication Data
Derrida, Jacques.
    Mémoires : for Paul de Man.
    (The Wellek Library lectures at the University of
California, Irvine)
    Includes index.
    1. De Man, Paul—Contributions in criticism—
Addresses, essays, lectures. 2. Criticism—Addresses,
essays, lectures. I. De Man, Paul. II. Title.
III. Series.
PN75.D45D47   1986   801'.95   85-27999
    ISBN 0-231-06232-X (alk. paper)

Columbia University Press
New York   Guildford, Surrey
Copyright © 1986 Columbia University Press
All rights reserved

Printed in the United States of America

Editorial Note

The Wellek Library Lectures are given annually at the University of California, Irvine, under the auspices of the Focused Research Program in Critical Theory and with the support of the Graduate Division. They are published with the generous assistance of Kendall E. Bailes, Dean of the School of Humanities, in conjunction with the Irvine Studies in the Humanities, which is under the general editorship of Robert Folkenflik.

These three lectures were translated by Cecile Lindsay, Jonathan Culler, and Eduardo Cadava, respectively. We are grateful to these translators, who worked independently of one another, and to Avital Ronell and Eduardo Cadava, who brought the translations of the individual lectures into conformity.

Focused Research Program in Critical Theory
Murray Krieger, Director

CONTENTS

PREFACE

THESE THREE LECTURES were written
a few weeks following the death of Paul de Man, between January and February, 1984. They were first delivered in French, at Yale University in March; and then,
a few weeks later, they were presented as part of the
René Wellek Library Lectures at the University of California, Irvine. The first lecture was delivered a second
time in English at Miami University (in Oxford, Ohio) at
a conference organized around the work of Paul de
Man. The conference was set up by James Creech and
Peggy Kamuf, bringing together Neil Hertz, Andrew Par-
ker and Andrzej Warminski. I wanted to produce these
details in order to thank all those who encouraged me
to write these pages and emboldened me to do so at
such a difficult moment; but also to stress another point:
in view of the time that has since elapsed, discussions
following these lectures, advice given me explicitly or
implicitly by those named above, by the translators, by
Cynthia Chase, and by Avital Ronell; in view, moreover,
of the recent publication of texts by Paul de Man which

at the time I did not know (in particular the essays on Hölderlin collected in *The Rhetoric of Romanticism,* Columbia University Press, 1984), I ought perhaps to have refined, inflected, complicated some of my assertions—and in more than one instance. I left this undone. Except to indicate specific bibliographical references. I have had to justify to myself with a number of reasons, which I entrust to the reader's understanding, having left these lectures in their original if somewhat rough state. On the one hand, I felt pressed to leave these texts with the special accent of their date, commanded by the fervor of bereaved friendship. One will not give finishing touches to sentences written under such circumstances. And then, particularly as regards Hölderlin, I know that the exchanges emerging from my suggestions (whether in the mode of private letters or debates in the course of the colloquium at Miami University) will give rise to excellent publications by those whom I name above. They, to my view, will lend precision to what I here set forth.

To all those who have translated and edited these texts, to those who have heard and discussed them, I wish to express my profound gratitude.

J.D.
21 December 1984

When first given in French at Yale University in the Bingham Hall library (Department of Comparative Literature), these lectures were preceded by these few words.

A PEINE

A peine—translation will continue to remain the subject of our seminar this year, as has been the case for the past five years. A peine: a scene is concealed within this French idiom, à peine, which already defies translation.

Rodolphe Gasché has spoken very well of Paul de Man's thought in terms of *Setzung* and of *Übersetzung* (*Diacritics*, Winter, 1981). But we would risk losing the essential point of that which he wished to say and Paul de Man wished to say if we translated *Übersetzung*. We would be overlooking the rapport between *Setzen* (the posing of the position, of *thesis* and *nomos*) and *Übersetzung* (trans- and superposing, sur-passing and over-exposing, passing beyond position). We would hardly be translating *Übersetzen* by translating if we translated it to translate.

But, already, how would one translate *à peine*? If one translated *à peine* by the equivalent of *presque* or rather *presque pas* (scarcely, hardly, almost not) or by the equivalent of "tout près de rien" (nearly not or nearly no) one would lose by the wayside the name or noun of *peine*, which virtually takes shelter, is hidden, almost disappearing, even for a French ear lulled a bit by that which we call "ordinary language." In the expression *à peine*, the French would hardly have heard the hard, the dash or the pain, the difficulty that there is or the trouble that one gives oneself. "Hardly" might be the best approximation. The French ear hardly perceives the sense of hardly.

To be able hardly to say something, hardly to begin this evening, hardly to recommence, repeat, or continue means to be able only with difficulty, with the pain of à peine—the affliction of hardly's hardship: hardly able, almost not to be able to, almost no longer able to say something, to begin, recommence and continue. This having trouble; with trouble, troubled and pained, it is hard even hardly to do, think or say that which however is said, thought, or done. Having trouble, being pained, as one would say in French, following.

This evening we can do hardly that which nonetheless we can—and must do. Not without going to pains. We speak and we think *here* for Paul de Man, with Paul de Man. But without him.

Here: a place, more than a library, something other than a classroom; we shall never be able to name, use, or recognize it without thinking of Paul de Man, his presence; his absence.

Each time, beginning so many years ago, when I spoke here he will have been there. And, for many among you, so many other times as well.

And it is hard for me to think that henceforth it should be otherwise. I can hardly think and speak otherwise henceforth.

I shall speak, therefore, of *Mémoires*.

Mémoires will be the title for this series of lectures. *Mémoires* in the plural, but also at once in the masculine and the feminine. The meaning of this word changes in French according to its generic determination (masculine/feminine) or its number (singular/plural). That is one of its singularities, and thus a theme of this seminar since, as we shall see confirmed, *Mémoires* is hardly translatable. That is why I prefer to speak here in my language, as usual, but I shall soon deliver these lectures in English at the University of California, Irvine.

For tonight's lecture I have chosen as subtitle "Mnemosyne."

(26 March 1984)

Tr. A.R.

MEMOIRES

for Paul de Man

I.

MNEMOSYNE

Translated by Cecile Lindsay

I have never known how to tell a story. And since I love nothing better than remembering and Memory itself—Mnemosyne—I have always felt this inability as a sad infirmity. Why am I denied narration? Why have I not received this gift? Why have I never received it from Mnemosyne, *tes tôn Mousôn metros*, the mother of all muses, as Socrates recalls in the *Theaetetus* (191b)? The gift (*doron*) of Mnemosyne, Socrates insists, is like the wax in which all that we wish to guard in our memory is engraved in relief so that it may leave a mark, like that of rings, bands, or seals. We preserve our memory and our knowledge of them; we can then speak of them, and do them justice, as long as their image (*eidolon*) remains legible.

But what happens when the lover of Mnemosyne has not received the gift of narration? When he doesn't know how to tell a story? When it is precisely because he keeps the memory that he loses the narrative?

I am not offering a rhetorical invocation to Mnemosyne.

Nor to a Remembrance (*Mémoire*) that one might naïvely believe to be oriented toward the past, a past whose essence one would learn through some narrative. My desire is to talk to you today about what is to come, about that future which, still to come, also comes to us from Paul de Man. Reading Proust, he said himself that "the power of memory" is not, first of all, that of "resuscitating": it remains enigmatic enough to be preoccupied, so to speak, by a thinking of "the future."

I had to commit to memory a proper name today. With the proper name Mnemosyne, I also wanted to recall the title of a poem by Hölderlin. A poem of mourning, to be sure, and about impossible mourning; a poem in mourning's default: when mourning is required, when it is requisite. I quote here several lines from the second version of "Mnemosyne":

Ein Zeichen sind wir, deutungslos
Schmerzlos sind wir und haben fast
Die Sprache in der Fremde verloren
Un signe, nous voilà, nul de sens
Nuls de souffrance nous voilà, et presque
    nous avons
Perdu notre langue au pays étranger. (tr.
Armel Guerne)[1]
A sign we are, unreadable
We are without pain and have almost
Lost language in the foreignness.
    . . . Denn nicht vermögen
Die Himmlischen alles. Nämlich es reichen
Die Sterblichen eh' an den Abgrund. . . .
    . . . Ils ne peuvent pas tout
Eux-mêmes les célestes. Car les mortels ont
    bien avant
Gagné l'abîme. . . . (tr. Armel Guerne)
. . . Because the heavenly ones
Are not capable of all. Namely mortals
Are closer to the abyss. . . .
    . . . da ging
Vom Kreuze redend, das
Gesetz ist unterwegs einmal
Gestorbenen, auf der schroffen Strass
Ein Wandersmann mit
Dem andern, aber was ist dies?
. . . tout là haut,
Parlant de cette croix plantée
En souvenir d'un mort, une fois,
En chemin, sur cette haute route
Un voyageur s'avance, encoléré
Par son pressentiment lointain
De l'autre, or qu'est cela? (tr. Armel Guerne,
    who seems to combine the second
    and third versions)

Là-bas où s'en va sur la haute route, parlant
De cette croix au bord du chemin plantée
En souvenir des morts,
Un voyageur avec l'autre.
Mais qu'est-ce donc? (tr. Gustave Roud)
Remembering one departed, once,
On the steep path, a Wanderer advances
Moved by his distant premonition
Of the other—but what is this? (tr. A.
Ronell)

I prefer to conclude by citing the third version, for it
names Mnemosyne:

.... Und es starben
Noch andere viel. Am Kithäron
    aber lag
Eleutherä, der Mnemosyne Stadt.
    Der auch als
Ablegte den Mantel Gott das
    abendliche nachher löste
Die Locken. Himmlische nemlich
    sind
Unwillig, wenn einer nicht die
    Seele schonend sich
Zusammengenommen, aber er
    musse doch; dem
Gleich fehlet die Trauer.
Et tant d'autres encore
Sont morts. Mais sur le bord du Cithéron
Git Eleuthères, cité de Mnémosyne
Qui elle aussi, comme le dieu du soir lui
    avait retiré
Son manteau, perdit ses boucles peu après.
Car les célestes sont
Indignés quand quelqu'un, sans preserver
    son âme

Se donne tout entier, qui cependant devait le
    faire;
A celui-là le deuil fait defaut. (tr. Armel
    Guerne;
    Gustave Roud has no translation for this
    version)
And many others died. But by
    Cithaeron, there stood
Eleutherae, Mnemosyne's town.
    From her also
When God laid down his festive
    cloak, soon after did
The powers of Evening sever a
    lock of hair. For the
Heavenly, when
    Someone has failed to collect
his soul, to spare it,
Are angry, for still he must;
    like him
Mourning is in default. (tr. Michael
    Hamburger; modified)

What is an impossible mourning? What does it
tell us, this impossible mourning, about an essence of
memory? And as concerns the other in us, even in this
"distant premonition of the other," where is the most
unjust betrayal? Is the most distressing, or even the
most deadly infidelity that of a *possible mourning* which
would interiorize within us the image, idol, or ideal of
the other who is dead and lives only in us? Or is it that
of the impossible mourning, which, leaving the other
his alterity, respecting thus his infinite remove, either
refuses to take or is incapable of taking the other within
oneself, as in the tomb or the vault of some narcissism?

These questions will not cease to haunt us. Pres-
ently we will read what Paul de Man leads us to think
concerning "true 'mourning.'"

But then why begin by quoting Hölderlin? For at least three reasons, which also belong to memories. Paul de Man was a great and fervent reader of Hölderlin, and his knowledge comprehended all the philological and hermeneutical debates which developed around both the poetic and the political history of German thought since the beginning of the century. Paul de Man's contribution makes up a part of these debates, notably through his contestation of a certain Heideggerian appropriation of Hölderlin's poetics. This duel is all the more striking since for Paul de Man, as for Heidegger, the figure of Hölderlin retains a sort of sacred singularity, even if Paul de Man does make the following accusation of Heidegger: "Hölderlin is the only one whom Heidegger cites as a believer cites holy writ" ("Heidegger's Exegeses of Hölderlin," *Blindness and Insight*, p. 250). Like a categorical imperative of reading, Hölderlin's voice commands from both Heidegger and de Man a sort of absolute respect, although not necessarily a movement of identification. It is precisely at the moment of the *law* that Paul de Man intends to rescue Hölderlin from appropriation-by-identification, from what might be called Heidegger's hermeneutic mourning. In *Wie Wenn Am Feiertage* . . . , Heidegger would have violently and unjustly identified "Natur" (*Die mächtige, die göttlich schöne Natur*) with *physis* and with Being, according to his familiar gesture, but also with the law (*Gesetz*: "*Nach vestem Geseze, wie einst, aus heiligen Chaos gezeugt*"). However, according to Paul de Man, on this point as well as on others, " . . . Hölderlin says exactly the opposite of what Heidegger makes him say" (pp. 254–55). The sentence is trenchant, direct, and courageous; moreover, it is underlined. I recognize its tone as that of certain judgments taking the form of defiance—what might be called de Manian provocation: "When he

states the law, the poet does not say Being, then, but
rather, the impossibility of naming anything but an
order that, in its essence, is distinct from immediate
Being" (p. 261). I do not know whether one ought to arbitrate
here between Heidegger and Paul de Man. I will not
take that risk, especially not within the limits of a lecture. The problem is approached from another point of
view by Suzanne Gearhart in her rigorous and lucid
study of Paul de Man, "Philosophy *Before* Literature:
Deconstruction, Historicity, and the Work of Paul de
Man."[3] I shall refer you to it frequently. For my part, I
shall simply stress one point here: the impossibility of
reducing a thinking of the law to a thinking of Being,
and the impossibility of naming without in some way
appealing to the order of the law. As early as 1955, this
is what Paul de Man felt he had to oppose to a certain
Heideggerian reading of Hölderlin. This thinking of the
law was always, with Paul de Man, a rigorous, enigmatic, paradoxical, and vigilant one. And I believe that
this thinking runs through all his work, like a fidelity
that was also a fidelity to Hölderlin. One can find signs
of this in the altogether original meditations on the contract, the promise, and the juridical or political performative which are also readings of Rousseau and Nietzsche
in *Allegories of Reading*.

The second reason why I wanted to begin by
naming Mnemosyne and Hölderlin comes like an order
I received from I don't know where, I don't know what
or whom; but let us say from the law which speaks to
me through memory. Forgive me for letting my own
memory speak here. I promise not to do it too often,
and I only give in to the impulse now because it again
concerns Hölderlin, Heidegger, and Paul de Man. When

I was preparing these lectures, Avital Ronell sent me from California the copy of *Blindness and Insight* that I had lent her in Paris, the copy that Paul de Man had dedicated to me in October 1971. Opening the book—it was after Paul's death, then—I discovered two pages written in his hand, two fragments of Hölderlin's poems patiently transcribed for me. They returned to me from America, like a memory of Hölderlin in America. And I remember the circumstances in which this gift had been given to me. It was during the course of a seminar that lasted for three years, revolving around *The Thing* (*La Chose*)—this was the title of the seminar—and *The Thing* according to Heidegger. It was Paul de Man who reminded me or often made me aware of Heidegger's more or less open allusions to Hölderlin, those coded and barely disguised types of *topoi* that initiates or accomplices recognize easily, and which form at once the originary debt, the law, and the very environment of a certain Heideggerian diction. Thus it is for the "bridge" (in *Bauen Wohnen Denken*), which is the example of that "thing" which "has its way of gathering close by itself earth and sky, divinities and mortals." At the beginning of a passage on which I dwelt at length, Heidegger calls the bridge "light and powerful" (*leicht und kräftig*). He puts quotation marks around the words but cites no reference, since their origin is so transparent. He even omits the quotation marks around certain words that belong to Hölderlin. Heidegger writes: "The bridge swings lightly and strongly over the river" ("Die Brücke schwingt sich 'leicht und kräftig' über der Strom"). In the poem I received from Paul's hand and which returned to me from America, Hölderlin writes the following: "Over the river, where gleaming it passes your site/lightly and strongly the bridge vaults" (Friedrich

Hölderlin, *Poems and Fragments,* tr. Michael Hamburger, University of Michigan Press, 1967). Paul de Man had added to this poem, entitled *Heidelberg,* the transcription of another fragment, taken from the first version of *Patmos:* here there is another bridge, this time above the abyss (*über den Abgrund*). But above what abyss? This poem, whose opening is in every heart and on everyone's lips ("Near is/And difficult to grasp, the God./ But where danger threatens/ That which saves from it also grows."), can also be read as a poem of mourning: "After that he dies. Much could/ Be said of it. And the friends at the very last/ Saw him, the gladdest, looking up triumphant./ yet they were sad, now that evening had come, amazed,/ For the souls of these men contained/ Things greatly predetermined, but under the sun they loved/ This life. . . ." And in the fragment Paul sent me in his own hand, the quotation stopped with these words: "And the most loved/ Live near, growing faint/ On mountains most separate./ Give us thus innocent water,/ O pinions give us, of sense most faithful/ To go over there and to return."

Today I understand more clearly than ever why, almost thirty years ago, one of Paul de Man's friends had called him "Hölderlin in America." He confided this to me one day—and that was my third reason.

I have never known how to tell a story. Why didn't I receive this gift from Mnemosyne? From this complaint, and probably to protect myself before it, a suspicion continually steals into my thinking: who can really tell a story? Is narrative possible? Who can claim to know what a narrative entails? Or, before that, the memory it lays claim to? What is memory? If the essence of memory maneuvers between Being and the law, what sense does it make to wonder about the being

and the law of memory? These are questions that cannot be posed outside of language, questions that cannot
be formulated without entrusting them to transference
and translation, above the abyss. For they require, from
one language to another, impossible passageways: the
fragile resistance of a span. What is the meaning of the
word "mémoire(s)" in French, in its masculine and
feminine forms (*un mémoire, une mémoire*); and in its
singular and plural forms (*un mémoire, une mémoire,*
and *des mémoires*). If there is no meaning outside memory, there will always be something paradoxical about
interrogating "*mémoire*" as a unit of meaning, as that
which links memory to narrative or to all the uses of the
word "*histoire*" (story, history, *Historie, Geschichte,* etc.).

Paul de Man often stresses the "sequential" and
"narrative" structure of allegory.[4] In his eyes, allegory is
not simply one form of figurative language among others; it represents one of language's essential possibilities: the possibility that permits language to say the
other and to speak of itself while speaking of something
else; the possibility of always saying something other
than what it gives to be read, including the scene of
reading itself. This is also what precludes any totalizing
summary—the exhaustive narrative or the total absorp-
tion of a memory. I have thus always thought that de
Man smiled to himself when he spoke of the narrative
structure of allegory, as if he were secretly slipping us a
definition of narration that is at once ironic and allegorical—a definition which, as you know, scarcely advances the story.

Among the stories that I will never know how to
tell, no matter how much I want to, is the story of all the
journeys that have led me here. Not only those which
have for a long time drawn me to America, but specifi-

cally those which bring me here today, after the invitation with which you honored me and the promise I made four years ago: to give three lectures in the Irvine Wellek Library Lecture Series. Two problems arose for me concerning titles. First, the title of the lecture series itself; I had initially read it as the irony of defiance, without knowing precisely on which side the greatest insolence lay. Since then, reading a particular text by René Wellek, "Destroying Literary Studies,"[5] might have prevented me from accepting such a patronage for these lectures. I am not at all referring to the way in which I am treated in the article, but rather to the judgments pronounced against Paul de Man and several others who are in my eyes, on the contrary, the honor and the chance, today, of those "literary studies." I will say nothing here about that text; I will discuss it in a long endnote (note 5) to the published version of this lecture. But I invite you to read that text. It seems to me one worthy of immortalizing its author, if indeed that remained to be done. Upon reflection, I decided to keep my promise, to accept the symbolic patronage of these lectures dedicated to the memory of my friends Paul de Man and Eugenio Donato, in order to demonstrate thereby on which side—their side—is situated not insolence but tolerance, the taste for reading and well-argued discussion, the refusal of arguments resting on authority and academic dogmatism. In short, to borrow Wellek's own words, the pursuit of "the very concepts of knowledge and truth" that he accuses us of destroying.

While the title of the series was not chosen by me, it nonetheless fell to me to choose one for these lectures. As of last summer, I had not yet found one. I discussed this with David Carroll and Suzanne Gearhart in order to ask their advice. They appeared to approve emphatically, it seemed to me, the first possibility that occurred to me, which was to analyze the different modes in which I perceived, experienced, and interpreted what a work that has since been published has called "Deconstruction in America."[6] This is the locus of a debate which is all the rage, as you know, at least in some academic circles. And, as you can imagine, the subject is of some interest to me. It is one worth taking up dispassionately, and should be approached from every analytical avenue possible, drawing on any available clue. Why did I then abandon the subject? For at least three or four reasons, but I will here indicate only their general nature.

In the first place, the clues are too numerous. I am not relating their excess to the limits imposed by three lectures of one hour apiece, but rather to the essential and thus uncontrollable overdetermination of the phenomenon. What is called or calls itself "deconstruction" also contains, lodged in some moment of its process, an auto-interpretive figure which will always be difficult to subsume under a meta-discourse or general narrative. And deconstruction can impose its necessity, if at all, only to the extent that, according to a law that can be verified in many analogous situations, it accumulates within itself those very forces that try to repress it. But it accumulates these forces without being able to totalize them, like those surplus values from which a victim of aggression always profits; for here totalization is exactly what an account, a story, and a narrative are denied. We recognize here one of the themes—which is also a gesture—of deconstructive discourse. How could a narrative account for a phenomenon in progress? This particular phenomenon also proceeds like a set of narratives which could have no closure, and which would be exceedingly difficult to situate. Geopolitics does not suffice. Can we speak of "deconstruction in America"? Does it take place in the United States? First in Europe, and then in America—as some too quickly conclude, thereby raising the questions (which are themselves not without interest) of reception, translation, appropriation, etc? Do we know first of all what deconstruction represents in Europe? We cannot know without drawing out all the threads of a knot where we see tangled with each other the history of philosophies, the histories of "Philosophy," of literatures, of sciences, of technologies, of cultural and university institutions, and of socio-political history and the structure of a multitude of linguistic or so-called personal idioms. These entanglements are multiple; they meet nowhere, neither in a point nor in a memory. There is no singular memory. Furthermore, contrary to what is so often thought, deconstruction is not exported from Europe to the United States. Deconstruction has several original configurations in this country, which in turn—and there are many signs of this—produce singular effects in Europe and elsewhere in the world. We would have to examine here the power of this American radiation in all its dimensions (political, technological, economic, linguistic, editorial, academic, etc.). As Umberto Eco noted in an interview in the newspaper *Libération* (August 20–21, 1983), deconstruction in Europe is a sort of hybrid growth and is generally perceived as an American label for certain theorems, a discourse, or a school. And this can be verified, especially in England, Germany, and Italy. But is there a proper place, is there a proper story for this thing? I think it consists only of transference, and of a thinking through of transference, in all the senses that this word acquires in more than one language, and first of all that of the transference between languages. If I had to risk a single definition of deconstruction, one as brief, elliptical, and economical as a password, I would say simply and without overstatement: *plus d'une langue*—both more than a language and no more of *a* language. In fact it is neither a statement nor a sentence. It is sententious, it makes no sense if, at least as Austin would have it, words in isolation have no meaning. What makes sense is the sentence. How many sentences can be made with "deconstruction"?

Deconstructive discourses have sufficiently questioned, among other things, the classical assurances of history, the genealogical narrative, and periodizations of all sorts, and we can no longer ingenuously propose a tableau or a history of deconstruction. Similarly, no matter what their interest or their necessity may be today, the social sciences (notably those dealing with cultural or scientific and academic institutions) cannot, as such, claim to "objectify" a movement which, essentially, questions the philosophical, scientific, *and* institutional axiomatics of those same social sciences. Even if, for the sake of convenience, we wanted to take an Instamatic photo of deconstruction in America, we would have to simultaneously capture all of its aspects. Its *political* aspects (they appear more and more clearly, both in the world and in political discourse itself, or at the frontier between the political, the economic, and the academic. This frontier is original to the United States; to envision the stakes involved, one need only read what is said about deconstruction in the *Wall Street Journal*, the *New Yorker*, or the *New York Review of Books*); its *ethical* aspects (it is in the name of morality and

against the corruption of academic mores that the most
venomous—and sometimes also the most obscuran-
tist—discourses are directed against deconstruction;
which does not exclude the faith, the rigorous ethical
sense, and even what we might call the Puritan integrity
of certain partisans of deconstruction); its *religious*
aspects (I think it is impossible to understand American
forms of deconstruction without taking into account
the various religious traditions, their discourses, their
institutional effects, and above all their academic effects; while opposition to deconstruction is often made
in the name of religion, we see at the same time the
development of a powerful, original, and already quite
diversified movement that calls itself "deconstructive
theology")[7]; its *technological* aspects (without taking
into account the obvious fact that deconstruction is inseparable from a general questioning of *tekhné* and technicist reasoning, that deconstruction is nothing without
this interrogation, and that it is anything *but* a set of
technical and systematic procedures, certain impatient
Marxists nevertheless accuse deconstruction of deriving
its "power" from the "technicality of its procedure"[8]);
and its *academic* aspects (in the sense of "professionalization"—it is not by chance that deconstruction has
accompanied a critical transformation in the conditions
of entry into the academic professions from the 1960s to
the 1980s—and also in the sense of the "division of
labor" between departments, a division whose classic
architecture has also been put into question; for deconstruction is also, and increasingly so, a discourse
and a practice *on the subject of* the academic institution,
professionalization, and departmental structures that
can no longer contain it. And when professional philosophers feign concern over the progress of deconstruc-

tion in literature departments, even to the point of indicting the philosophical naïveté of the poor literary scholar, you can easily conclude—and immediately verify—that what makes Searle and Danto and others so nervous is what is happening all around them, to *their* colleagues, assistants, or students *in philosophy departments*). For the other aspects, I will simply say "etc.": the schema remains the same.

The second reason why I decided not to talk about "deconstruction in America," disregarding the advice of Suzanne Gearhart and David Carroll, is that one cannot and should not attempt to survey or totalize the meaning of an ongoing process, especially when its structure is one of transference. To do so would be to assign it limits which are not its own; to weaken it, to date it, to slow it down. For the moment, I do not care to do this. To make "deconstruction in America" a theme or the object of an exhaustive definition is precisely, by definition, what defines the enemy of deconstruction— someone who (at the very least out of ambivalence) would like to wear deconstruction out, exhaust it, turn the page. You can well understand that in this matter I am not the one in the greatest hurry.

The third reason: I will only state its form. As I will say tomorrow about memory and the word "mémoire"—and for exactly the *same reasons*—there is no sense in speaking of *a* deconstruction or *simply* deconstruction as if there were only one, as if the word had a (single) meaning outside of the sentences which inscribe it and carry it within themselves.

The fourth reason is that of a singular circle, one which is "logical" or "vicious" in appearance only. In order to speak of "deconstruction in America," one would have to claim to know what one is talking about, and first of all what is meant or defined by the word "America." Just what is America in this context? Were I not so frequently associated with this adventure of deconstruction, I would risk, with a smile, the following hypothesis: America *is* deconstruction (l'Amérique, mais *c'est* la deconstruction). *In this hypothesis,* America would be the proper name of deconstruction in progress, its family name, its toponymy, its language and its place, its principal residence. And how could we define the United States *today* without integrating the following into the description: It is that historical space which today, in all its dimensions and through all its power plays, reveals itself as being undeniably the most sensitive, receptive, or responsive space of all to the themes and effects of deconstruction. Since such a space represents and stages, in this respect, the greatest concentration *in the world,* one could not define it without at least including this symptom (if we can even speak of symptoms) in its definition. In the war that rages over the subject of deconstruction, there is no front; there are no fronts. But if there were, they would all pass through the United States. They would define the lot, and, in truth, the partition of America. But we have learned from "Deconstruction" to suspend these always hasty attributions of proper names. My *hypothesis* must thus be abandoned. No, "deconstruction" is not a proper name, nor is America the proper name of deconstruction. Let us say instead: deconstruction and America are two open sets which intersect partially according to an allegorico-metonymic figure. In this fiction of truth, "America" would be the title of a new novel on the history of deconstruction and the deconstruction of history.

This is why I have decided not to talk to you

about "deconstruction in America." As of December, I
still did not have a title for these three lectures.

After the death of Paul de Man on December 21, a
necessity became clear to me: I would never manage
to prepare these lectures, I would have neither the
strength nor the desire to do so, unless they left or gave
the last word to my friend. Or at least, since that had
become literally impossible, to friendship, to the unique
and incomparable friendship that ours was for me,
thanks to him. I could only speak *in memory of him.*
In memory of him: these words cloud sight and
thought. What is said, what is done, what is desired
through these words: *in memory of . . .*?

I will speak of the future, of what is bequeathed
and promised to us by the work of Paul de Man. And, as
you shall see, this future is not foreign to *his* memory; it
keeps to what he said, thought, and affirmed *on the
subject of* memory. Yes: affirmed. And I see this affirmation of memory, without which the friendship of which
I am speaking would never have taken place, in the
form of a ring or an *alliance.* This alliance is much more
ancient, resistant, and secret than all those strategic or
familial manifestations of alliance that it must actually
make possible and to which it is never reduced. In the
said context of "deconstruction in America," there have
certainly been several apparently strategical alliances
between Paul de Man and some of his friends. To analyze these would be interesting, necessary, and difficult,
but such an analysis could not be only a socioinstitu-
tional one. And we would understand nothing about
what *comes to pass and takes place* if we did not account
for this affirmation which comes to seal an alliance. An
alliance which is not secret because it would be pro-
tected behind some clandestine, occult "cause" in want

of power, but because the "yes," which is a non-active act, which states or describes nothing, which in itself neither manifests nor defines any content, this *yes* only commits, before and beyond everything else. And to do so, it must repeat itself to itself: *yes, yes*. It must preserve memory; it must commit itself to keeping its own memory; it must promise itself to itself; it must bind itself to memory for memory, if anything is ever to come from the future. This is the law, and this is what the performative category, in its current state, can merely approach, at the moment when "yes" is said, and "yes" to that "yes."

It is this affirmation from Paul de Man that I would attempt calling or recalling—recalling to myself—with you today. What binds it to memory, to a thinking through of thinking memory, is also the measure and chance of his future.

Such an affirmation is not foreign to that which, as I have so often repeated, resides at the heart of deconstruction. In speaking to you today of Paul de Man, in speaking in memory of Paul de Man, I will therefore not be entirely silent on the question of "deconstruction in America." What would it have been without him? Nothing; or something entirely different—this is too evident for me to insist on. But just as, under the name or in the name of Paul de Man, we cannot say *everything* about deconstruction (even in America), so I cannot, in such a short time and under the single title of memory, master or exhaust the immense work of Paul de Man. Let us call it allegory or double metonymy, this modest journey that I will undertake for a few hours with you.

It is a modest journey, but one that is magnetized by the alliance between memory and the seal of the "yes, yes," as well as by Paul de Man's signature. Or at least by certain traits of such a paraph. The paraph is only a schematic and marginal countersignature, a fragment of signature; indeed, who can claim to decipher a whole signature? Re-reading this "yes" in memory of itself, I especially wish to denounce the sinister ineptitude of an accusation—that of "nihilism"—which so many major professors, following the example of minor journalists, have often made against Paul de Man and his friends. Underlying and beyond the most rigorous, critical, and relentless irony, within that *"Ironie der Ironie"* evoked by Schlegel, whom he would often quote, Paul de Man was a thinker of affirmation. By that I mean—and this will not become clear immediately, or perhaps ever—that he existed himself in memory of an affirmation and of a vow: yes, yes.

What does this mean? What do we mean by "in memory of" or, as we also say, "to the memory of"? For example, we reaffirm our fidelity to the departed friend by acting in a certain manner *in memory of* him, or by dedicating a speech *to his memory*. Each time, we know our friend to be gone forever, irremediably absent, annulled to the point of knowing or receiving nothing himself of what takes place in his memory. In this terrifying lucidity, in the light of this incinerating blaze where nothingness appears, we remain in *disbelief* itself. For never will we believe either in death or immortality; and we sustain the blaze of this terrible light through devotion, for it would be unfaithful to delude oneself into believing that the other living *in us* is living *in himself:* because he lives *in us* and because we live this or that in his memory, in memory of him.

This being "in us," the being "in us" of the other, in bereaved memory, can be neither the so-called resurrection of the other *himself* (the other is dead and noth-

ing can save him from this death, nor can anyone save
us from it), nor the simple inclusion of a narcissistic
fantasy in a subjectivity that is closed upon itself or even
identical to itself. If it were indeed a question of narcissism, its structure would remain too complex to allow
the other, dead or living, to be reduced to this same
structure. Already installed in the narcissistic structure,
the other so marks the self of the relationship to self, so
conditions it that the being "in us" of bereaved memory
becomes the *coming* of the other, a coming of the other.
And even, however terrifying this thought may be, the
first coming of the other.

Let us not again take up the discussion of mourning or the so-called work of mourning. We have all spoken, written, and argued a great deal about it, especially
in these last few years. It will not surprise you when I
say that all I have recently read and reread by Paul de
Man seems to be traversed by an insistent reflection on
mourning, a meditation in which bereaved memory is
deeply engraved. Funerary speech and writing do not
follow upon death; they work upon life in what we call
autobiography. And this takes place between fiction and
truth, *Dichtung und Wahrheit.* In "Autobiography as De-
facement" (*MLN*, 1979, reprinted in *The Rhetoric of Romanticism,* p. 67), a discussion takes place on the undecidable distinction between fiction and autobiography. But of course this undecidability itself remains
untenable:

. . . the distinction between fiction and autobiography is not
an either/or polarity but . . . it is undecidable. But is it possible to remain, as Genette would have it, *within* an undecidable situation? As anyone who has ever been caught in a revolving door can testify, it is certainly most uncomfortable,
and all the more so in this case since this whirligig [the

"tourniquet" that Genette speaks of in relation to fiction and autobiography in Proust] is capable of infinite acceleration and is, in fact, not successive but simultaneous. A system based on two elements that, in Wordsworth's phrase, "of these [are] neither, and [are] both at once" is not likely to be sound (p. 70).

Why this long quotation? Specifically, in order to announce that motif of infinite acceleration which, as we shall see, by gathering memory into a moment, by contracting the times of the "yes" into the point of an affirmation that wants to be indivisible, at times confuses two figures that Paul de Man judges at once inseparable and irreducible: *irony* and *allegory*. In this particular text, the problem of autobiography *seems* to elicit several concerns: that of *genre,* of *totalization,* and of the *performative* function. And these three concerns are linked to a certain relationship to memory or to memoirs. First concern, *genre:* "By making autobiography into a genre, one elevates it above the literary status of mere reportage, chronicle, or *memoirs* [my emphasis—J.D.] and gives it a place, albeit a modest one, among the canonical hierarchies of the major literary genres" (p. 67). After which it will be demonstrated that autobiography is neither a genre nor a mode, but "a figure of reading . . . that occurs in all texts" since a "specular structure" is always "interiorized" there. Second concern, *totalization*: far from assuring any identification with the self or any gathering around the self, this specular structure reveals a tropological dislocation that precludes any anamnesic totalization of self:

The specular moment that is part of all understanding reveals the tropological structure that underlies all cognitions, including knowledge of self. The interest of autobiography, then, is not that it reveals reliable self-knowledge—it does not—but that it demonstrates in a striking way the impossibility of closure and of totalization (that is, the impossibility of coming into being) of all textual systems made up of tropological substitutions (p. 71).

And, finally, the *performative* function: as soon as the gathering of Being and totalizing memory are impossible, we recognize the fatality of this tropological dislocation, which is another turn of memory, another twist of memory. And this fatality is the law, or let us say instead, the law of the law: the moment when the authority of the law comes to take turns with, as if it were its own supplement, the impossible gathering of Being. In terms of speech acts, the law takes the form of the performative, be it pure or impure. Whatever we may conclude on this subject, this is the reason that I began by situating a *différend* between Paul de Man and Heidegger concerning Hölderlin, Being, and the law. We have here a continuous trait that runs through all the mutations of the de Manian text, from 1955 to 1979, and, as we shall see, up to 1983. "Autobiography as Defacement" reveals—notably through a critical analysis of Philippe Lejeune's book—the necessity of a passage from ontological identity and knowledge to resolution, action, and promise; to legal authority and the performative function. But it also demonstrates the inevitable temptation to reinscribe the tropology of the subject in a specular mode of knowledge which displaces, without surmounting, another specularity:

For just as autobiographies, by their thematic insistence on the subject, on the proper name, on *memory,* on birth, eros, and death, and on the doubleness of specularity, openly declare their cognitive and tropological constitution, they are equally eager to escape from the coercions of this system. Writers *of* autobiographies as well as writers *on* autobio-

graphies are obsessed by the need to move from cognition to
resolution and to action, from speculative to political and
legal authority. Philippe Lejeune, for example . . . stubbornly
insists . . . that the identity of autobiography is not represen-
tational and cognitive but contractual, grounded not in
tropes but in speech acts. . . . The fact that Lejeune uses
"proper name" and "signature" interchangeably signals both
the confusion and the complexity of the problem. For just as
it is impossible for him to stay within the tropological system
of the name and just as he has to move from ontological
identity to contractual promise, as soon as the performative
function is asserted, it is at once reinscribed within cognitive
constraints (p. 71; my emphasis on *memory*—J.D.).

The rest of the argument, which I cannot trace
here, reveals several types of specular pairs as well as
the fatal necessity of "reentering a system of tropes at
the very moment we claim to escape from it." I said a
moment ago that this problem of memoirs or of the
autobiographical memory was *apparently* informed by
the three concerns of genre, totalization, and performative language. Beyond this preliminary appearance,
what is precisely at stake is a tropology of memory in
autobiographical discourse *as* epitaph, as the signature
of its own epitaph—if something of this sort were possible other than through a figure, trope, or fiction. What
figure? What fiction? What trope? *Prosopopeia*. The
"autobiographical text" that de Man judges here as
"exemplary" is Wordsworth's *Essays on Epitaphs*, which,
from a discourse *on the subject of* epitaphs, comes to be
itself an epitaph, "and more specifically, the author's
own monumental inscription or autobiography." I prefer to let you read or reread these pages by Paul de Man
on your own. They are magnificent, and are illumined
by the dark light of the sun, ironically accomplishing in

their turn what they pretend to attribute simply, and precisely, to Wordsworth. They become in their turn, by doing what they tell of and by telling what they do, Paul de Man's epitaph, the prosopopeia that he addresses to us from an incineration all the more sublime for having no tomb—emblazoned spirit, glorious beyond the tomb and its sepulchral inscriptions. Here is the figure, the visage, the face and the *de-facement,* the effacement of the visible figure in prosopopeia: the sovereign, secret, discrete, and ideal signature—and the most giving, the one which *knows how to efface itself.* The whole scene is oriented toward this conclusion: "The dominant figure of the epitaphic or autobiographical discourse is, as we saw, the prosopopeia, the fiction of the voice-from-beyond-the-grave; an unlettered stone would leave the sun suspended in nothingness" (p. 77). This fiction of voice, this "fictional voice," Paul de Man will later say, takes the form of an *address.* From his demonstration, I only quote this sort of theorem of prosopopeia, which, figuratively addressed to us, looks at us, describes and prescribes to us, dictates to us in advance, with the voice and under the initialed signature of Paul de Man, what we are doing here and now: to be sure, making a pro-sopopeia, sacrificing to fiction—and what he reminds us of is that prosopopeia remains a fictive voice, al-though I believe that this voice already haunts any said real or present voice. But we are sacrificing to fiction through love for him, and in his name, in his naked name, in memory of him. In the movement of this trope, we turn toward him, we address ourselves to him, who addresses himself to us. And love's movement counts no less than its having arrived at its destination, at the right address:

... the epitaph, says Wordsworth, "is open to the day; the sun looks down upon the stone, and the rains of heaven beat against it." The sun becomes the eye that reads the text [here again, *en abîme*, is an example of what Paul de Man calls the "allegory of reading"; this allegory seems to me to hold all the privilege (which is itself allegorico-metonymic) of the sun, and, as Ponge would say, of the sun placed *en abîme*] of the epitaph. And the essay tells us what this text consists of, by way of a quotation from Milton that deals with Shakespeare: "What need'st thou such weak witness of thy name?" In the case of poets such as Shakespeare, Milton or Wordsworth himself, the epitaph can consist only of what he calls "the naked name" (p. 133), as it is read by the eye of the sun. At this point, it can be said of "the language of the senseless stone" that it acquires a "voice," the *speaking* stone counterbalancing the *seeing* sun. The system passes from sun to eye to language as name and as voice. We can identify the figure that completes the central metaphor of the sun and thus completes the tropological spectrum that the sun engenders: it is the figure of prosopopeia, the fiction of an apostrophe to an absent, deceased or voiceless entity, which posits the possibility of the latter's reply, and confers upon it the power of speech. Voice assumes mouth, eye, and finally face, a chain that is manifest in the etymology of the trope's name, *prosopon poiein*, to confer a mask or a face (*prosopon*). Prosopopeia is the trope of autobiography, by which one's name, as in Milton's poem, is made as intelligible and *memorable* [my emphasis—J.D.] as a face. Our topic deals with the giving and taking away of faces, with face and deface, *figure*, figuration and disfiguration. (pp. 75–76)

"Central metaphor," "tropological spectrum": the figure of prosopopeia looks back and keeps in memory, we could say, clarifies and recalls in Paul de Man's last texts, everything that he signed, from "The Rhetoric of Temporality" to *Allegories of Reading*. As if the scene of

the epitaph and of prosopopeia had imposed itself upon
him in the last years of his life. But he demonstrates to
us that this is a scene from which poetic discourse cannot escape. The prosopopeia of prosopopeia that I have
just recalled dates from 1979. In 1981, in "Hypogram
and Inscription, Michael Riffaterre's Poetics of Reading"
(*Diacritics*, Winter, 1981), prosopopeia becomes "the
master trope of poetic discourse" (p. 33), "the very figure of the reader and of reading." This admirable argument gives us much to think about concerning the
hypographic signature and what we call "hallucination" ["prosopopeia is hallucinatory" (p. 34)]; it also
situates the abyss of a "prosopopeia of prosopopeia" (p.
34).

   Is it possible, when one is in memory of the
other, in bereaved memory of a friend, is it desirable to
think of and to pass beyond this hallucination, beyond a
prosopopeia of prosopopeia? If death exists, that is to
say, if it happens and happens only once, to the other
and to oneself, it is the moment when there is no longer
any choice—could we even think of any other—except
that between memory and hallucination. If death comes
to the other, and comes to us through the other, then the
friend no longer exists except *in* us, *between* us. In himself, by himself, of himself, he is no more, nothing more.
He lives only in us. But *we* are never *ourselves*, and between us, identical to us, a "self" is never in itself or
identical to itself. This specular reflection never closes
on itself; it does not appear *before* this *possibility* of
mourning, before and outside this structure of allegory
and prosopopeia which constitutes in advance all
"being-in-us," "in-me," between us, or between ourselves. The *selbst*, the *soi-même*, the self appears to itself
only in this bereaved allegory, in this hallucinatory
prosopopeia—and even before the death of the other

actually happens, as we say, in "reality." The strange situation I am describing here, for example that of my friendship with Paul de Man, would have allowed me to say all of this *before* his death. It suffices that I know him to be mortal, that he knows me to be mortal—there is no friendship without this knowledge of finitude. And everything that we inscribe in the living present of our relation to others already carries, always, the signature of *memoirs-from-beyond-the-grave.* But this finitude, which is also that of memory, does not at first take the form of a *limit,* of a limited ability, aptitude, or faculty, of a circumscribed power. Nor does it assume the form of a limit which would move us to multiply testamentary signs, traces, hypograms, *hypomnemata,* signatures and epigraphs, or autobiographical "memoirs." No, this finitude can only take that form through the trace of the other in us, the other's irreducible precedence; in other words, simply the trace, which is always the trace of the other, the finitude of memory, and thus the approach or remembrance of the future. If there is a finitude of memory, it is because there is something of the other, and of memory as a memory of the other, which comes from the other and comes back to the other. It defies any totalization, and directs us to a scene of allegory, to a fiction of prosopopeia, that is, to tropologies of mourning: to the memory of mourning and to the mourning for memory. This is why there can be no *true mourning,* even if truth and lucidity always presuppose it, and, in truth, take place only as the truth of mourning. The truth of the mourning of the other, but of the other who always speaks in me before me, who signs in my place, the hypogram or epitaph being always of the other, and for the other. Which also means: in the place of the other.

It is perhaps for this reason, because there is no

"true" mourning, that Paul de Man puts quotation
marks around the word "mourning" when he speaks of
"true 'mourning.'" It is "mourning" that he places in
quotation marks, not "true." But he does this in a text
("Anthropomorphism and Trope in the Lyric," also reprinted in *The Rhetoric of Romanticism,* p. 239) which
begins with a quotation from Nietzsche: "Was ist also
Warheit? Ein beweglicher Heer von Metaphern,
Metonymien, Anthropomorphismen." ("What is truth
then? A mobile army of metaphors, metonymies, and
anthropomorphisms.") The "truth" of "true 'mourning'" is also part of the procession; it follows or precedes the theory of figures, and this rhetoricity is in no
way a part of a consoling simulacrum. I would even say
that in this procession mourning takes on the full gravity of its meaning: it is born from it; it endures and
remains in sufferance there. Here are the last lines of the
essay which opened with the quotation from Nietzsche;
they conclude a very rich comparative analysis of Baudelaire's poems "Obsession" and "Correspondances":

> Generic terms such as lyric (or its various sub-species, ode,
> idyll or elegy) as well as pseudo-historical period terms such
> as romanticism or classicism are always terms of *resistance*
> and nostalgia, at the furthest remove from the *materiality of
> actual history.* If mourning is called a "chambre d'éternel deuil
> où vibrent de vieux râles" [a chamber of eternal mourning
> vibrating with old death rattles—"Obsession"], then this pa-
> thos of terror states in fact the desired consciousness of eter-
> nity and of temporal harmony as voice and as song. True
> "mourning" is less deluded. The most *it* can do is to allow for
> non-comprehension and enumerate non-anthropomorphic,
> non-elegiac, non-celebratory, non-lyrical, non-poetic, that is
> to say prosaic, or, better, *historical* modes of language power.
> (p. 262)

    I underlined in passing the words "resistance"

and "materiality of actual history." De Manian criticism or deconstruction is always, also, an analysis of "resistances" and of the symptoms they produce (for example, the "resistance to theory" in literary studies). As for history, that is another theme of these lectures, and I will return to it shortly.

What, then, is true "mourning"? Paul de Man does not say that it is possible in the traditional sense of truth; he does not say that it is truly possible or possible at present. True "mourning" seems to dictate only a tendency: the tendency to accept incomprehension, to leave a place for it, and to enumerate coldly, almost like death itself, those modes of language which, in short, deny the whole rhetoricity of the true (the non-anthropomorphic, the non-elegiac, the non-poetic, etc.). In doing so, they also deny, paradoxically, the *truth* of mourning, which consists of a certain rhetoricity—the allegorical memory which constitutes any trace as always being the trace of the other. I do not know if death teaches us anything at all, but this is what we are given to consider by the experience of mourning, which begins with the "first" trace, that is, "before" perception, on the eve of meaning, leaving no chance for any innocent desire for truth.

What, then, is *true mourning*? What can we make of it? Can we *make it*, as we say in French that we "make" our mourning? I repeat: "can we?" And the question is double: are we *capable* of doing it, do we have the *power* to do it? But also, do we have the *right*? Is it right to do so? Is it also the *duty* and movement of fidelity? We are back to the question of Being and the law, at the heart of memory. If this experience of memory, of the memorial, of the memorandum, and of memoirs encounters mourning, who could think that this would be accidental? This experience is mournful in its very essence; it gathers itself together, it assembles itself to contract alliance with itself, only in the impossible affirmation of mourning. But this impossible affirmation must be possible: this singular affirmative affirmation *must* affirm the impossible, without which it is only a report, a technics, a recording. The impossible here is the other, such as he comes to us: as a mortal, to us mortals. And whom we love as such, affirming this to be good.

Earlier we asked the question: what do we mean by "in us" when, speaking at the death of a friend, we declare that from now on everything will be situated, preserved, or maintained in us, only "in us," and no longer on the other side, where there is nothing more. All that we say of the friend, then, and even what we say *to him*, to call or recall him, to suffer for him with him—all that remains hopelessly *in* us or *between* us the living, without ever crossing the mirror of a certain speculation. Others would speak too quickly of a totally interior speculation and of "narcissism." But the narcissistic structure is too paradoxical and too cunning to provide us with the final word. It is a speculation whose ruses, mimes, and strategies can only succeed in supposing the other—and thus in relinquishing in advance any *autonomy*. On the question of Narcissus and the aforementioned narcissism, it will one day be necessary to read (and I am sure that someone will) those infinitely complicated texts on narcissism; namely, Freud's "On Narcissism: An Introduction," together with all the numerous and inexhaustible texts in which Paul de Man puts Narcissus back in play. And if they both were to say that Narcissus is an allegory, this should not be taken as a scholarly banality.

Everything remains "in me" or "in us," "between us," upon the death of the other. Everything is entrusted *to me;* everything is bequeathed or given *to us,* and first of all *to* what I call memory—*to the memory,* the place of this strange dative. All we seem to have left is memory, since nothing appears able to come to us any longer, nothing is coming or to come, from the other to the present. This is probably true, but is this truth true, or true enough? The preceding sentences seem to suppose a certain clarity in respect to what we mean by "in me," "in us," "death of the other," "memory," "present," "to come," and so on. But still more light (*plus de lumière*) is needed. The "me" or the "us" of which we speak then arise and are delimited in the way that they are only through this experience of the other, and of the other as other who can die, leaving in me or in us this memory of the other. This terrible solitude which is mine or ours at the death of the other is what constitutes that rela- tionship to self which we call "me," "us," "between us," "subjectivity," "intersubjectivity," "memory." The *possibility* of death "happens," so to speak, "before" these different instances, and makes them possible. Or, more precisely, the possibility of the death of the other *as* mine or ours in-forms any relation to the other and the finitude of memory.

We weep *precisely* over what happens to us when everything is entrusted to the sole memory that is "in me" or "in us." But we must also recall, in another turn of memory, that the "within me" and the "within us" *do not* arise or appear *before* this terrible experience. Or at least not before its possibility, actually felt and inscribed in us, signed. The "within me" and the "within us" acquire their sense and their bearing only by carrying within themselves the death and the memory of the other; of an other who is greater than them, greater than what they or we can bear, carry, or comprehend, since we then lament being no more than "memory,"

"in memory." Which is another way of remaining in-
consolable before the finitude of memory. We know, we
knew, *we remember*—before the death of the loved one—
that being-in-me or being-in-us is constituted out of the
possibility of mourning. We are only ourselves from the
perspective of this knowledge that is older than ourselves; and this is why I say that we begin by *recalling*
this to ourselves: we come to ourselves through this
memory of *possible* mourning.

In other words, this is precisely the allegory, this
memory of impossible mourning. Paul de Man would
perhaps say: of the *unreadability* of mourning. The possibility of the impossible commands here the whole
rhetoric of mourning, and describes the essence of
memory. Upon the death of the other we are given to
memory, and thus to interiorization, since the other,
outside us, is now nothing. And with the dark light of
this nothing, we learn that the other resists the closure
of our interiorizing memory. With the nothing of this
irrevocable absence, the other appears *as* other, and as
other for us, upon his death or at least in the anticipated
possibility of a death, since death constitutes and makes
manifest the limits of a *me* or an *us* who are obliged to
harbor something that is greater and other than them;
something *outside of them within them.* Memory and interiorization: since Freud, this is how the "normal"
"work of mourning" is often described. It entails a
movement in which an interiorizing idealization takes
in itself or upon itself the body and voice of the other,
the other's visage and person, ideally *and* quasi-literally
devouring them. This mimetic interiorization is not fictive; it is the origin of fiction, of apocryphal figuration.
It takes place in a body. Or rather, it makes a place for a
body, a voice, and a soul which, although "ours," did

not exist and had no meaning *before* this possibility that one *must* always begin by remembering, and whose trace must be followed. *Il faut,* one *must:* it is the law, that law of the (necessary) relation of Being to law. We can only live this experience in the form of an aporia: the aporia of mourning and of prosopopeia, where the possible remains impossible. Where *success fails.* And where faithful interiorization bears the other and constitutes him in me (in us), at once living and dead. It makes the other a *part* of us, between us—and then the other no longer quite seems to be the other, because we grieve for him and bear him *in us,* like an unborn child, like a future. And inversely, the *failure succeeds:* an aborted interiorization is at the same time a respect for the other as other, a sort of tender rejection, a movement of renunciation which leaves the other alone, outside, over there, in his death, outside of us.

Can we accept this schema? I do not think so, even though it is *in part* a hard and undeniable necessity, the very one that makes *true mourning* impossible.

The chance of a single idiom has it that memory and interiorization coincide in *Erinnerung.* In German it means remembrance, and Hegel notes its motif of subjectivizing interiorization. In French, I would be tempted to propose a new usage of the word *"intimation,"* whose artifice could signal, at once, the intimacy of an interiority and the open order or injunction (in French, we intimate an order, we give it: *il faut,* one *must*).

In the last few years, Paul de Man had worked, taught, and written on the subject of the opposition posited by Hegel's *Encyclopedia* between *Erinnerung* and *Gedächtnis,* between remembrance as interiorization and a thinking memory which can also be linked to

technical and mechanical hypomnesis. In an essay entitled "Sign and Symbol in Hegel's *Aesthetics*" (*Critical
Inquiry,* Summer 1982), the analysis of this opposition
(between *Erinnerung* and *Gedächtnis*) is articulated with
that of the symbol and the sign, leading back in conclusion to the motif of allegory which was probably one of
the most sustained in Paul de Man's thought. Both enigmatic and inescapable, this motif is like the unique and
plural touchstone by which all readings and all literary
and philosophical corpuses are measured. The allegory
to which we are led again is, on the one hand, the
Hegelian concept of allegory as it is presented in the
lectures of the *Aesthetics;* on the other hand, it is also
Hegelian philosophy *as allegory,* in the very special sense
given to the term by Paul de Man: that of a sort of
narrative (rather than historical) fable—or rather, that
of a story which certain people know how to tell about
something which, finally, is not historical. Taking this
text as my point of departure, I will speak about this in
my next lecture. For the moment I will say only that it is
Hegelian allegory—that allegory which constitutes the
grand final figure of philosophy and of the philosophy
of history, that absolute memory and absolute knowledge—which will also be, in Paul de Man's paradox, the
figure of every *disjunction* between philosophy and history, between literature and aesthetics, and between literary experience and literary theory. This conclusion
may seem surprising as a conclusion, deprived as it
is at present of its demonstration; but it also concerns
the resistance to literary theory, a resistance which
Paul de Man analyzes from the perspective of a politico-
institutional concern to which we will return later: "No
wonder that literary theory has such a bad name, all the
more so since the emergence of thought and of theory is

not something that our thought [*Gedächtnis,* in contrast to interiorizing memory, *Erinnerung*] can hope to prevent or to control." These are the last words of that text.

An uncontrollable necessity, a *nonsubjectivizable* law of thought beyond interiorization, beyond the unmourning thought of mourning: how can we accept that? And why should we affirm it? This can no longer even become a question.

When we say "in us" or "between us" to recall ourselves faithfully "to the memory of," of which memory are we speaking, *Gedächtnis* or *Erinnerung?* The movement of interiorization keeps within us the life, thought, body, voice, look or soul of the other, but in the form of those hypomnemata, memoranda, signs or symbols, images or mnesic representations which are only lacunary fragments, detached and dispersed—only "parts" of the departed other. In turn they are parts of us, included "in us" in a memory which suddenly seems greater and older than us, "greater," beyond any quantitative comparisons: sublimely greater *than* this other that the memory harbors and guards within it, but also greater *with* this other, greater than itself, inadequate to itself, pregnant with this other. And the figure of this bereaved memory becomes a sort of (possible and impossible) metonymy, where the part stands for the whole and for *more than* the whole that it exceeds. An allegorical metonymy, too, which says something other than what it says and manifests the other (*allos*) in the open but nocturnal space of the *agora*—in its *plus de lumière:* at once no more light, and greater light. It speaks the other and makes the other speak, but it does so in order to let the other speak, for the other will have spoken first. It has no choice but to let the other speak, since it cannot make the other speak without the other having *already* spoken, without this *trace* of speech which comes from the other and which directs us to writing as much as to rhetoric. This trace results in speech always saying something other than what it says: it says the other who speaks "before" and "outside" it; it lets the other speak in the allegory. Whence the structure of the "rhetoric of temporality." But what defies the simple and "objective" logic of sets, what disrupts the simple inclusion of a part within the whole, is what recalls itself beyond interiorizing memory (*Erinnerung*), is what recalls itself to thought (*Gedächtnis*) and *thinks itself* as a "part" which is greater than the "whole." It is the other as other, the non-totalizable trace which is in-adequate to itself and to the same. This trace is interiorized *in* mourning *as* that which can no longer be interiorized, as impossible *Erinnerung,* in and beyond mournful memory—constituting it, traversing it, exceeding it, defying all reappropriation, even in a coded rhetoric or conventional system of tropes, in the *exercises* of prosopopeia, allegory, or elegiac and grieving metonymy. But this exercise lies in wait for, and technique always feeds off of, the true Mnemosyne, mother of all muses and living source of inspirations. Mnemosyne can also become a poetic topos.

We *think* this. To this thought there belongs the gesture of faithful friendship, its immeasurable grief, but also its life: the sublimity of a mourning without sublimation and without the obsessive triumph of which Freud speaks. Or still again, "funeral monumentality" without "paranoid fear."[9]

In the strict and almost institutional domain of rhetoric, all figures, modes, or types—be they classifiable or unclassifiable—receive their (unclassifiable) possibility from these paradoxical structures: first, the inclusion in a set of a part that is greater than the set; second, a logic or an a-logic of which we can no longer say that it belongs to mourning in the current sense of the term, but which regulates (sometimes like mourning in the strict sense, but always like mourning in the sense of a general possibility) all our relations with the other *as other*, that is, as mortal for a mortal, with the one always capable of dying before the other. Our "own" mortality is not dissociated from, but rather also conditions this rhetoric of faithful memory, all of which serves to seal an alliance and to recall us to an affirmation of the other. The death of the other, if we can say this, is also situated on our side at the very moment when it comes to us from an altogether other side. Its *Erinnerung* becomes as inevitable as it is unliveable: it finds there its origin and its limit, its conditions of possibility and impossibility. In another context, I have called this Psyche: Psyche, the proper name of an allegory; Psyche, the common name for the soul; and Psyche, in French, the name of a revolving mirror. Today it is no longer Psyche, but apparently Mnemosyne. In truth, tomorrow, and the day after tomorrow, the "naked name" will be Paul de Man. This is what we shall call to, and toward which we shall again turn our thoughts.

Notes

1. *Blindness and Insight: Essays in the Rhetoric of Contemporary Criticism* (Minneapolis: University of Minnesota Press, 1983), p. 92.

2. I will also cite Gustave Roud's translation, which appears in the Pléiade edition of Hölderlin's work:

Un signe, tels nous sommes, et de sens nul
Morts à toute souffrance, et nous avons presque
Perdu notre langage en pays ètranger

. . .

Car les Maîtres du ciel n'ont point
Toute puissance. Oui, les mortels avant eux atteignent
Le bord du gouffre.

3. Published in *Diacritics* (Winter 1983), vol. 13 no. 4. This is one of the three texts on the work of Paul de man with which, without being able to cite them each time, I will, so to speak, dialogue obliquely but constantly throughout these three lectures. The discussion undertaken in this essay by Suzanne Gearhart concerns in depth all of Paul de Man's published work and raises notably, with great rigor, the question of the continuity or discontinuity between *Blindness and Insight* and *Allegories of reading*. This essay is also a discussion with Rodolphe Gasché, whose two texts, "Deconstruction as Criticism," *Glyph* 6 and "Setzung and Übersetzung: Notes on Paul de Man," *Diacritics* (Winter 1981), constitute undoubtedly today, to my knowledge, the most ample and penetrating reading of the de Manian text. As Suzanne Gearhart rightly remarks, a kind of displacement is at work in Gasché's perspective from one text to the next, and it is not without relation to what Gasché, as opposed to Suzanne Gearhart, interprets as a displacement within Paul de Man's work itself, between his two great books.

I want first of all to give credit to the authors of these three essential texts that any reader of Paul de Man will henceforth have to confront—texts that are therefore essential for me, and I here want to express my gratitude to their authors. But I will have to, in the course of the brief itinerary of these three lectures, refrain from quoting them and from taking part, at least directly, in the *explication* (debate) that is developed in them. By explication I do not mean "explication de texte" but rather *Auseinandersetzung*, a word that must be added as the measure of the other to the series *Setzung* and *Übersetzung*. *Auseinandersetzung* is to explain oneself to the other in a debate, a discussion, or even a *polemos*. If I refrain here from explicitly and literally taking part in this *Auseinandersetzung*, it is for several reasons.

(1) The *Auseinandersetzung* is too rich, too complex, too overdetermined for me to do it justice in lectures lasting only several hours. But what I will attempt to say on the subject of the de Manian text could afterward, I hope, from another point of view and without further detour, find the path of this *Auseinandersetzung*.

(2) This *Auseinandersetzung* is not only a debate with Paul de Man, it is also a critical *explication* between Suzanne Gearhart and Rodolphe Gasché. I have neither the means nor in truth the desire today to play referee or to count points—especially not here, for, given the subtlety and overdetermination of the texts in question and the rigor and exactingness of their authors, it

would be foolish to believe that one could be right or determine who is right here, to believe that the "true" is on one side or the other.

(3) Finally, the thing, *Die Sache,* of this *Auseinandersetzung* is even more complicated for them and for me given the fact that I don't have the natural position of an observer here. I am, one could say, party to the *Auseinandersetzung* even before having opened my mouth today. Not only because Paul de Man, Rodolphe Gasché, and Suzanne Gearhart are my friends, but because what I have written is part of the litigation. Neither am I able nor do I wish to act today as if I were in the position of being able to open or close the dossier of this case. The only lesson I wish to give today is the following: listen to what they say, learn to read Paul de Man, Rodolphe Gasché, Suzanne Gearhart.

4. Cf., for example: "Allegory is sequential and narrative, yet the topic of its narration is not necessarily temporal at all," in "Pascal's Allegory of Persuasion," *Allegory and Representation,* ed. by Stephen Greenblatt (Baltimore: Johns Hopkins University Press, 1981), p.1. The logic of this proposition supports his recurrent critique of all historicisms, all periodizations, all narratives of origin. He always treats them as figures of rhetoric, as fables or fictions. Allegories are narrative and narrations are allegorical.

5. *The New Criterion,* December 1983. This article takes on its full meaning within a specific conjuncture. It belongs to a series or to what we might call a campaign: certain professors invested with a great deal of prestige, and thus also with a great deal of academic power, launch a campaign against what seems to them to threaten the very foundation of this power—its discourse, its axiomatics, its procedures, its theoretical and territorial limits, etc. In the course of this campaign, they grasp at straws; they forget the elementary rules of reading and of philological integrity in whose name they claim to do battle. They think they can identify deconstruction as the common enemy. I recall what Paul de Man said on the subject of one of these maneuvers, that of Water Jackson Bate, Kingsley Porter University Professor at Harvard, which appeared in "The Crisis in English Studies" (*Harvard Magazine,* Sept./Oct. 1982). Paul de Man said that Professor Bate "has this time confined his sources of information to *Newsweek* magazine. . . . What is left is a matter of law enforcement rather than critical debate. One must be feeling very threatened indeed to become so aggressively defensive" ("The Return to Philology," *Times Literary Supplement,* December 10, 1982). I had pointed out elsewhere an essay belonging to the same series: "The Shattered Humanities" (*Wall Street Journal,* December 31, 1982) by the Chairman of the National Endowment for the Humanities. I did this last year in a lecture delivered in April ("The University in the Eyes of its Pupils," *Diacritics,* Fall 1983). Since then, the series has not stopped growing, and there is still the same refusal or inability in respect to a first task, the most elementary of tasks: that of reading. And the panicked dogmatism becomes more and more insulting; humor becomes increasingly rare; pieces of evidence are concealed. Philosophical

arguments are made on the basis of remarks reportedly heard at cocktail parties (for example, those attributed to Michel Foucault by John Searle in a recent piece in *Times Literary Supplement*, October 27, 1983); adversaries or their "disciples" are labeled "moonies," for example by Arthur Danto in a recent debate in *Times Literary Supplement* (September 30, 1983). All of this is not very important, but it must be taken seriously. A careful and meticulous analysis of all these symptoms, in the United States and elsewhere, teaches us much—and not only about what deconstruction can illuminate or displace in respect to academic culture and institutional politics. Recalling the attacks which converged against Paul de Man in recent years, I will simply refer here to the analyses that he made of them in "The Resistance to Theory," *Yale French Studies*, no. 63 (1982), and in the introduction to "Hegel and the Sublime" in *Displacements*, M. Krupnick, ed. (Bloomington: Indiana University Press, 1983). He must certainly not have read that passage by René Wellek (to whom he introduced me some ten years ago, to whom we ran into occasionally, and of whom we sometimes spoke, always in happy moments of shared good humor) where he is called a "gloomy" existentialist. Did Wellek read Paul de Man? Was he capable of it? It does not suffice, in order to know how to read, simply to own a library and to know how to talk. In saying this I am referring to what can be inferred about non-reading from another assertion by Wellek, according to which I supposedly advanced "the preposterous theory that writing precedes speaking, a claim refuted by every child and by the thousand spoken languages that have no written records." I quote this "child" argument not only because it demonstrates that the condemned texts have not even been opened, but because it feeds, directly or indirectly, *all* the articles whose convergence I noted above. Will Wellek have the honesty to admit his haste and superficiality? Bate had this honesty (to a certain degree, for his "auto-critique" still remains quite superficial and casual) when he admitted that "[My] short paragraph [!] on deconstruction was admittedly testy and unfairly dismissive. But I hasten to say that a close study of Culler's recent book helped to change my perspective and encouraged me to consider the subject with a less prejudiced mind. Accordingly, I wish I had omitted that paragraph." Fine; but the paragraph in question was indissociable from the whole of the argument, while this remark was published elsewhere, in a completely different type of journal, with other addressees, other effects, and another politico-academic scope. Like everything that is published in *Harvard Magazine, The New York Review of Books*, or *The Times Literary Supplement*. Bates, who wishes to belong to those "minorities" who "have strong voices," expresses his remorse in the form of a letter to the editor of *Critical Inquiry* (December 1983), after the publication of an excellent article by Stanley Fish ("Profession Despise Thyself: Fear and Self-Loathing in Literary Studies"). Fish accuses Bate, among other things, of setting himself up as the supreme judge on the subject of texts which he obviously had never read or which he knew only through *Newsweek* (Again! One day an accounting will have to be made of the role that these publications now play in an apparently academic debate).

6. Jonathan Arac, Wlad Godzich, Wallace Martin eds., *The Yale Critics: Deconstruction in America* (Minneapolis: University of Minnesota Press, 1983).

7. T. Althizer, M. Myers, C. Raschke, R. Scharleman, M. Taylor, C. Winquist, *Deconstruction and Theology* (New York: Continuum, 1982); Mark C. Taylor, *Deconstructing Theology* (New York: Crossroad, 1982); *Erring, A Postmodern A/Theology* (Chicago: University of Chicago Press, 1984); and a special issue of *Semeia* 23, Robert Detweiler, ed. *Derrida and Biblical Studies*, etc.

8. John Brenkman, "Deconstruction and the Social Text," *Social Text* (1979), :186–88. "Deconstruction . . . mirrors the effacement of ideology under the mantle of technical rationality which is the principal feature of ideology under late capitalism. . . . Deconstruction is the specular image of the society of the spectacle." Michael Sprinker, "The Ideology of Deconstruction: Totalization in the Work of Paul de Man," paper delivered at the MLA Convention (1980), Special Session on "Deconstruction as/of Politics," quoted in "Variations on Authority: Some Deconstructive Transformations of the New Criticism," Paul A. Bové, in *The Yale Critics: Deconstruction in America*, p. 3. All this in not false; it can become true here and there, and it concerns at any rate only *certain* ideological *exploitations* of deconstruction—exploitations which must be analyzed as such, in the context of what is calmly called here and elsewhere "late capitalism." It also comes to cover certain stereotyped formalizations of "late Marxism." Fortunately all marxisms are not reduced to this.

9. Paul de Man: "the uneasy combination of funereal monumentality with paranoid fear that characterizes the hermeneutics and the pedagogy of lyric poetry," "Anthropomorphism and Trope in the Lyric," *The Rhetoric of Romanticism* (New York: Columbia University Press, 1984), p. 259.

II.

THE ART OF
MÉMOIRES

Translated by Jonathan Culler

Yesterday, you may remember, we made each other a promise. I now recall it, but you already sense all the trouble we will have in ordering all these presents: these past presents which consist of the present of a promise, whose opening toward the present to come is not that of an expectation or an anticipation but that of commitment.

We had promised each other—but in truth I was the only one to do so—to call a name: Paul de Man: a "naked name": Paul de Man. In saying (here let me quote myself in French) "le 'naked name,' ce sera Paul de Man. C'est *lui* que nous appellerons, c'est vers *lui* que nous tournerons encore pensée," I deliberately took advantage of a language: my own. In French, at least, one cannot determine whether we would be turning our thoughts toward Paul de Man or toward his name. Was this merely indecorous play with a grammatical ambiguity? Or perhaps a magical incantation, uttered without many illusions, but as if, having become as one with his name in my memory, the departed friend would respond to the just call of his name, as if the impossibility of distinguishing Paul de Man from the name "Paul de Man" conferred a power of resurrection on naming itself, or better still, on the apostrophe of the call recalling "the naked name," as if any uttered name resuscitated resurrection: "Lazarus, arise!"—this is what the apostrophe to the naked name would say or stage.

But what Paul de Man tells us about address, apostrophe, and prosopopoeia, about its "tropological spectrum," forbids us to give in to magic here. We must nevertheless consider that which, in the structure or the power of the name, particularly the so-called proper name, awakens, calls for, attracts, or makes possible such magic: not only the desire but also the experience of hallucination.

What constrains us to think (without ever believing in it) a "true mourning" (if such there be) is the essence of the proper name. What in our sadness we call the life of Paul de Man is, in our memory, the moment when Paul de Man himself could answer to the name, Paul de Man, and answer in and for the name of Paul de Man. At the moment of death the proper name remains; through it we can name, call, invoke, designate, but we know, we can *think* (and this thought cannot be reduced to mere memory, though it comes from a memory) that Paul de Man himself, the bearer of the name and the unique pole of all these acts, these references, will never again answer to it, never himself answer, never again except through what we mysteriously call our memory.

I said yesterday that if I have chosen to speak to you of "memories" in memory of Paul de Man, it is doubtless to remain awhile longer near my friend, to keep watch over, take in, slow down, or annul the separation. But I do so also because "memory" was for Paul de Man a place (a topos or theme, as you wish) of original, continuing reflection, yet still generally hidden, it seems to me, from his readers. And since I wished not to discuss the entire oeuvre of Paul de Man but to follow, modestly, a single thread in it, a thread which would intersect in a modest, limited way with the thread of "deconstruction in America," I thought that the thread of memory could orient us in Paul de Man's thought and guide us during our passage in this allegorical labyrinth. Unless Ariadne's thread is also the thread spun by the Fates. Naturally, as you realize, "memories" here is not the name of a simple topos or identifiable theme; it is perhaps the focus, with no sacrosanct identity, of an enigma that is all the more difficult to decipher since it conceals nothing behind the appearance of a word but plays with the very structure of language and some remarkable surface effects.

"Memory" is first the name of something that I shall not define for the moment, singling out only this feature: it is the name of what for us (an "us" which I define only in this way) preserves an essential and necessary relation with the possibility of the name, and of what in the name assures preservation. Not preservation as what conserves or maintains the thing named: we have just seen on the contrary that death reveals the power of the name to the very extent that the name continues to name or to call what we call the bearer of the name, and who can no longer answer to or answer in and for his name. And since the possibility of this situation is revealed at death, we can infer that it does not wait for death, or that in *it* death does not wait for death. In calling or naming someone while he is alive, we know that his name can survive him and *already survives him*; the name begins during his life to get along without him, speaking and bearing his death each time it is pronounced in naming or calling, each time it is inscribed in a list, or a civil registry, or a signature. And if at my friend's death I retain only the memory and the name, the memory in the name, if something of the name flows back into pure memory because a certain function is defunct there, "defuncta," and because the other is no longer there to answer, this defect or default reveals the structure of the name and its immense power as well: it is in advance "in memory of." We cannot separate the name of "memory" and "memory" of the name; we cannot separate the name and memory. And this is not at all for the simple reason that the word "memory" is itself a name, although that, as we shall see in a moment, is not without interest.

But when we say that the name is "in memory of," are we speaking of every name, be it a proper name or a common noun? And does the expression "in memory of" mean that the name is "in" our memory—supposedly a living capacity to recall images or signs from the past, etc.? Or that the name is in itself, out there somewhere, like a sign or symbol, a monument, epitaph, stele or tomb, a memorandum, aide-mémoire, a memento, an exterior auxiliary set up "in memory of"? Both, no doubt; and here lies the ambiguity of memory, the contamination which troubles us, troubles memory and the meaning of "memory": death reveals that the proper name could always lend itself to repetition in the absence of its bearer, becoming thus a singular common noun, as common as the pronoun "I," which effaces its singularity even as it designates it, which lets fall into the most common and generally available exteriority what nevertheless *means* the relation to itself of an interiority.

With this we enter into the reading of the essay of Paul de Man's that I only mentioned in yesterday's lecture, "Sign and Symbol in Hegel's *Aesthetics*" (1982). It figures among the last that he published. I will cite several lines, somewhat mechanically, for memory's sake, for your memory; then we will distance ourselves for the time of a detour and return to them later. Should quotation make me hesitate—frequent and extensive quotation? Ultimately, at the very extremity of the most ambiguous fidelity, a discourse "in memory of" or "to the memory of" might even wish only to quote, always supposing that one knows where a quotation begins and where to end it. Fidelity requires that one quote, in the desire to let the other speak; and fidelity requires that one not just quote, not restrict oneself to quoting. It

is with the law of this double law that we are here engaged, and this is also the double law of Mnemosyne—
unless it is the common law of the double source,
Mnemosyne/ Lethe: source of memory, source of forgetting. They tell, and here is the enigma, that those con-
sulting the oracle of Trophonios in Boetia found there
two springs and were supposed to drink from each,
from the spring of memory and from the spring of forgetting. And if *Lethe* also names the allegory of oblivion,
of death or sleep, you will readily recognize in
Mnemosyne, its other, a figure of truth, otherwise called
aletheia.

    I must, then, quote but also interrupt quotations:

    1. The first of two quotations I chose because it
identifies a certain relationship between memory and
the name. Paul de Man had just recalled the opposition
between *Gedächtnis* and *Erinnerung* in Hegel's *Encyclopedia. Gedächtnis* is both the memory that thinks (and
moreover preserves in itself, literally, through the echo
in its very name, the memory of *Denken*) and voluntary
memory, specifically the mechanical faculty of memorization, while *Erinnerung* is interiorizing memory,
"recollection as the inner gathering and preserving of
experience" (p. 771). What interests Paul de Man above
all, what he emphatically underlines, is this strange col-
lusion in memory as *Gedächtnis* between thinking
thought and *tekhnè* at its most external, what would
seem the most abstract and spatial kind of inscription.

The question remains, however, whether the external manifestation of the idea, when it occurs in the sequential development of Hegel's thought, indeed occurs in the mode of
recollection, as a dialectic of inside and outside susceptible
of being understood and articulated. Where is it, in the
Hegelian system, that it can be said that the intellect, the

mind, or the idea leaves a material trace upon the world, and how does this sensory appearance take place?

The answer takes a hint from the same section (para. 458, p. 271) near the end of the *Encyclopedia* in a discussion on the structure of the sign, with which we began. Having stated the necessity to distinguish between sign and symbol and alluded to the universal tendency to conflate one with the other, Hegel next makes reference to a faculty of the mind which he calls *Gedächtnis* and which "in ordinary [as opposed to philosophical] discourse is often confused with recollection [*Erinnerung*] as well as with representation and imagination"—just as sign and symbol are often used interchangeably in such modes of ordinary discourse as literary commentary or literary criticism. . . . Memorization has to be sharply distinguished from recollection and from imagination. It is entirely devoid of images (*bildlos*), and Hegel speaks derisively of pedagogical attempts to teach children how to read or write by having them associate pictures with specific words. But it is not devoid of *materiality* altogether.

(I interrupt this quotation for a moment after having underlined the word *materiality.* There is a theme of "materiality," indeed an original materialism in de Man. It concerns a "matter" which does not fit the classical philosophical definitions of metaphysical materialisms any more than the sensible representations or the images of matter defined by the opposition between the sensible and the intelligible. Matter, a matter without presence and without substance, is what resists these oppositions. We have just placed this resistance on the side of thought, in its strange connivance with materiality. We might have associated it yesterday with death and with that allusion to "true 'mourning'" which makes a distinction between pseudo-historicity and "the materiality of actual history." Despite all his suspicions of historicism or historical rhetorics blind to their own rhetoricity, Paul de Man constantly contended with the irreducibility of a certain history, a history with which all one can do is to undertake its "true 'mourning.'" Let us recall: "Generic terms such as 'lyric' . . . as well as the pseudo-historical period terms such as 'romanticism' or 'classicism' are always terms of *resistance* and nostalgia, at the furthest remove from the *materiality of actual history*." The materiality of actual history is thus that which resists historical, historicizing resistance. De Man continues: "True 'mourning' is less deluded. The most *it* can do is to allow for non-comprehension and enumerate non-anthropomorphic, non-elegiac, non-celebratory, non-lyrical, non-poetic, that is to say prosaic, or, better, *historical* modes of language power." Matter of this sort, "older" than the metaphysical oppositions in which the concept of matter and materialist theories are generally inscribed, is, we might say, "in memory" of what precedes these oppositions. But by this very fact, as we shall see later, it retains an essential relation with fiction, figurality, rhetoricity. *Matière et Mémoire* is the title I could have given to this long parenthesis. One more quotation before I bring it to a close:

Gedächtnis, of course, means memory in the sense that one says of someone that he has a good memory but not that he has a good remembrance or a good recollection. One says, in German, "sie" or "er hat ein gutes Gedächtnis," and not, in that same sense, "eine gute Erinnerung." The French *mémoire,* as in Bergson's title *Matière et Mémoire,* is more ambivalent, but a similar distinction occurs between *mémoire* and *souvenir; un bon souvenir* is not the same as *une bonne mémoire* [ibid., p. 772].)

Closing this parenthesis, I take up once again my earlier citation where I left off, to offer now a justification for the title I have chosen for this lecture, "The Art of Memories," and to bring into view the crisscrossings of genitives or genealogies between the name of "memory" and the memory of the name.

> . . . But it [memory] is not devoid of materiality altogether. We can learn by heart only when all meaning is forgotten and words read as if they were a mere list of names. "It is well known," says Hegel, "that one knows a text by heart [or by rote] only when we no longer associate any meaning with the words; in reciting what one thus knows by heart one necessarily drops all accentuation."
>
> We are far removed, in this section of the *Encyclopedia* on memory, from the mnemotechnic icons described by Frances Yates in *The Art of Memory* and much closer to Augustine's advice about how to remember and to psalmodize Scripture. Memory, for Hegel, is the learning by rote of *names* [de Man's italics] or of words considered as names. . . .

De Man's stipulation seems crucial. It emphasizes not only that memory works better when dealing with lists of names learned by heart, but that everything that we know by heart and everything that strangely links memory as *Gedächtnis* to thought is of the order of the name. The name, or what can be considered as such, as having the function or power of the name—this is the sole object and sole possibility of memory, and in truth the only "thing" that it can at the same time both name and think. This means then that any name, any nominal function, is "in memory of"—from the first "present" of its appearance, and finally, is "in virtually-bereaved memory of" even during the life of its bearer.

> . . . and it can therefore not be separated from the notation, the inscription, or the writing down of these names [Remember what we were saying yesterday about the *Essays upon Epitaphs*]. In order to remember, one is forced to write down what one is likely to forget. The idea, in other words, makes

its sensory appearance, in Hegel, as the material inscription of names. Thought is entirely dependent on a mental faculty that is mechanical through and through, as remote as can be from the sounds and the images of the imagination or from the dark reach of words and of thought.

The synthesis between name and meaning that characterizes memory is an "empty link" [*das leere Band*] and thus entirely unlike the mutual complementarity and interpenetration of form and content that characterizes symbolic art. (pp. 772–73)

2. The second quotation, from the same text, does not directly concern the memory of the name but what one might call—and it comes to much the same thing—the forgetting of the pronoun, singularly of the first pronoun, the *I*. The effacing of the *I* in a kind of *a priori* and functional forgetting could be related to what we said yesterday of "Autobiography as De-facement." But we should also bear in mind the consequence—one among many—of this effacement of the *I* for the classical theory of the performative. An "explicit" performative seems to require the absolute priority of utterances—in the first person singular (with a verb in the present tense of the active voice). This privilege of the *I* is even sometimes extended to so called "primary" (rather than explicit) performatives.[1] Now here is what Paul de Man concludes from an analysis of Hegel's famous and "odd sentence" "Ich kann nicht sagen was ich (nur) meine," where the final word, as many have noted, plays on the verb *meinen* (to mean, but also to have a *Meinung* or personal opinion) and the possessive pronoun, *mein, meine,* so that ultimately "what the sentence actually says is 'I cannot say I.'" It would take too much time to set forth the analysis itself, and in any case what interests me here is Paul de Man's move rather than Hegel's:

The mind has to recognize, at the end of its trajectory—in this case at the end of the text—what was posited at the beginning. It has to recognize itself as itself, that is to say, as I. But how are we to recognize what will necessarily be erased and forgotten, since "I" is, per definition, what *I* can never say? (p. 770)

And three pages further on:

In memorization, in thought, and, by extension, in the sensory manifestation of thought as an "art" of writing, "we are dealing only with signs [wir haben es überhaupt nur mit Zeichen zu tun]." Memory effaces remembrance (or recollection) *just as the I effaces itself.* (p. 773, my italics)

I emphasize the *I*'s effacement of itself and the *just as,* which does not in fact juxtapose two analogous possibilities. It is the *same* possibility. The same necessity as well, which makes the inscription of memory an effacement of interiorizing recollection, of the "living remembrance" at work in the presence of the relation to self. We suggested yesterday that this eclipse or ellipsis in the movement of interiorization is due not to some external limit or finite limitation of memory but to the structure of the relation to the other, as to the always allegorical dimension of mourning.

Paul de Man's thesis, if one may call it that (we will come back to this shortly), is that the relation between *Gedächtnis* and *Erinnerung,* between memory and interiorizing recollection, is not "dialectical," as Hegelian interpretation and Hegel's interpretation would have it, but one of rupture, heterogeneity, disjunction.

Memory is the name of what is no longer only a mental "capacity" oriented toward one of the three modes of the present, the past present, which could be dissociated from the present present and the future present. Memory projects itself toward the future, and it constitutes the presence of the present. The "rhetoric of temporality" *is* this rhetoric of memory. Paul de Man was less and less inclined to describe it in dialectical terms—and it remains to be seen whether the Husserlian and Heideggerian analyses of the movement of temporalization would provide any essential help (I deliberately leave this question open for the moment). The "dialecticizing" style seems more marked, for example, in a given passage of his reading of Blanchot reading Mallarmé ("Impersonality in Blanchot" in *Blindness and Insight,* pp. 70–71), though even there I have doubts. It is certainly not in this style that de Man writes here of memory as a tension toward the future, or even as a relation to the presence of the present. The failure or finitude of memory says something about truth, and about the truth of memory: its relation to the other, to the instant and to the future.

. . . Poulet had stated that "the major discovery of the eighteenth century was the phenomenon of memory," yet it is the concept of instantaneity that finally emerges, often against and beyond memory, as the main insight of the book. The *instant de passage* supplants memory or, to be more precise, supplants the naive illusion that memory would be capable of conquering the distance that separates the present from the past moment. . . . Memory becomes important as failure rather than as achievement and acquires a negative value. . . . The illusion that continuity can be restored by an act of memory turns out to be merely another moment of transition. (*Blindness and Insight,* pp. 90–91)

The failure of memory is thus not a failure; we can also interpret its apparent negativity, its very finitude, what affects its experience of discontinuity and distance, as a power, as the very opening of difference, indeed of an ontological difference (ontic-ontological: between Being and beings, between the presence of the present and the present itself). If this were the case, what would happen when this *ontological difference* is translated into the *rhetoric of memory*? Or vice versa? Can one speak in this case of a simple equivalence or of a correlation that could be read in one direction or the other? Let us allow this question the opportunity to remain open; it was never posed as such by Paul de Man.

If memory gives access to this difference, it does not do so simply by way of the classical (originally Hegelian) schema that links the essence of a being to its past being (*être-passé*), *Wesen* to *Gewesenheit.* The memory we are considering here is not essentially oriented toward the past, toward a past present deemed to have really and previously existed. Memory stays with traces, in order to "preserve" them, but traces of a past that has never been present, traces which themselves never occupy the form of presence and always remain, as it were, to come—come from the future, from the *to come.* Resurrection, which is always the formal element of "truth," a recurrent difference between a present and its presence, does not resuscitate a past which had been present; it engages the future.

In this memory which promises the resurrection of an anterior past, a "passé antérieur," as we say in French to designate a grammatical tense, Paul de Man always saw a kind of formal element, the very place where fictions and figures are elaborated. If one allowed oneself to hazard a summary no less unjust than economical, no less provocative than hasty, one could say that for Paul de Man, great thinker and theorist of memory, there is only memory but, strictly speaking, the past does not exist. It will never have existed in the present, never been present, as Mallarmé says of the present itself: "un présent n'exists pas." The allegation of its supposed "anterior" presence *is* memory, and is the origin of all allegories. If a past does not literally exist, no more does death,[2] only mourning, and that other allegory, including all the figures of death with which we people the "present," which we inscribe (among ourselves, the living) in every trace (otherwise called "survivals"): those figures strained toward the future across a fabled present, figures we inscribe because they can outlast us, beyond the present of their inscription: signs, words, names, letters, this whole text whose legacy-value, as we know "in the present," is trying its luck and advancing, *in advance* "in memory of . . . "

Paul de Man was always attentive to this trace of the future as the power of memory, as he was to the fiction of anteriority. Reading Poulet reading Proust, he notes,

The power of memory does not reside in its capacity to resurrect a situation or a feeling that actually existed, but is a constitutive act of the mind bound to its own present and oriented toward the future of its own elaboration. The past intervenes only as a purely formal element. . . . The transcendence of time . . . has freed itself from a rejected past, but this negative moment is now to be followed by a concern with the future that engenders a new stability, entirely distinct from the continuous and Bergsonian duration of memory. (*Blindness and Insight,* p. 92–93)

In speaking of a present that will never have been present, have I distorted de Man's thought, pushing it to an extreme? The passage I have just cited does not *literally* say this. It affirms that memory does not have to resuscitate what "actually existed" but it does not deny the

"actual existence." This is true, of course, but what if
memory of this sort were *already* at work in the relation
of the present itself to its own presence? What if there
were a *memory of the present* and that far from fitting the
present to itself, it divided the instant? What if it inscribed or revealed difference in the very presence of the
present, and thus, by the same token, the possibility of
being repeated in representation? Bringing together the
Nietzschean and Baudelairian conceptions of modernity, Paul de Man cites "Le Peintre de la vie moderne,"
the text Baudelaire devotes to Constantin Guys: "Le
plaisir que nous retirons de la représentation du présent
tient non seulement à la beauté dont il peut être revêtu,
mais aussi à sa qualité essentielle de présent" ("The
pleasure we derive from the *representation of the present*
is not merely due to the beauty it may display, but also
to the essential 'present-ness' of the present." "Literary
History and Literary Modernity," in *Blindness and Insight,* p. 156). By translating "qualité essentielle de présent" by "present-ness of the present," ones makes the
reader more attentive to the ontological difference, to
the essence, to the difference between the simple present and the presence of the present. This difference is
never by definition present; it arises only for memory,
but for memory as "memory of the present." The passage continues:

The paradox of the problem is potentially contained in the
formula "représentation du présent," which combines a re-
petitive with an instantaneous pattern without apparent
awareness of the incompatibility. Yet this latent tension gov-
erns the development of the entire essay. Baudelaire remains
faithful throughout to the seduction of the present; any temporal awareness is so closely tied for him to the present moment that memory comes to apply more naturally to the
present than it does to the past:

Woe be to him who, in antiquity, studies anything besides
pure art, logic and general method! By plunging into the
past he may well lose the memory of the present (*la
mémoire du présent*). He abdicates the values and privi-
leges provided by actual circumstances, for almost all our
originality stems from the stamp that time prints on our
sensations.
(Malheur à celui qui étudie dans l'antiquité autre chose
que l'art pur, la logique, la méthode générale! Pour s'y trop
plonger, il perd la mémoire du présent; il abdique la valeur
et les privilèges fournis par les circonstances; car presque
toute notre originalité vient de l'estampille que le *temps*
imprime à nos sensations.)
The same temporal ambivalence prompts Baudelaire to couple any evocation of the present with terms such as "représentation," "mémoire," or even "temps," all opening per-
spectives of distance and difference within the apparent uni-
queness of the instant. Yet his modernity too, like Nietzsche's,
is a forgetting or a suppression of anteriority.

In trying too hard to recall or plunge into the
past, one forgets the present, says Baudelaire, who
wants thus to save both memory and the present, that
memory of the present which recalls the present to its
own presence, that is to say, to its difference: to the
difference which makes it unique by distinguishing it
from the other present *and* to that quite different difference which relates a present to presence itself. Only a
memory can recognize this differential "stamp," this
mark or signature, this patent or trademark that "time
prints on our sensations." Neither time nor memory is
anything other than the figure of these marks. And this
"memory of the present" only marks itself, and this
mark arrives only to efface the anteriority of the past.
Memory, and "Yet," de Man says, "a forgetting or a
suppression of anteriority." The sentence beginning
with "Yet" concerns, of course, "modernity"—Baude-

laire's or Nietzsche's—but it describes at the same time a figure whose necessity has imposed its law on the most diverse de Manian readings. I will never say on *all* his readings—on principle: never, but especially not in these three modest efforts, would I attempt totalization in the face of an oeuvre that has so often uncovered, analyzed, denounced, and avoided it.

Despite the interval (of time) that separates these two texts, we can now bring together this last formulation, memory as "a forgetting or a suppression of anteriority," and the formulation previously encountered in the essay on Hegel, "Memory effaces remembrance." We will come back to this after a detour to note several other motifs.

The first, which seems to me also very persistent, if not highly visible, in the most diverse movements of de Manian interpretation, is that of acceleration, of an absolute precipitousness. These words do not designate a particular rhythm, a measurable or comparable speed, but a movement which attempts through an infinite acceleration to win time, to win over time, to deny it, one might say, but in a non-dialectical fashion, since it is the form of the instant that is charged with the absolute discontinuity of this rhythm without rhythm. This acceleration is incommensurable, and thus infinite and null at the same time; it touches the sublime.[3]

Among many possible examples let me cite, from the same essay, the passage which seems to describe the Monsieur Guys of Paul de Man's Baudelaire. Here, where de Man says of Baudelaire that he says of Guys what in truth he says of himself, in his name and for himself, how can one avoid reading in this passage something Paul de Man is having said by these two others about himself, for himself, in his name, through the effects of an irony of the signature? Irony or allegory of the trademark (stamp, *estampille*), perhaps? We shall come back to this. For the moment—and here is my second motif, which can also be pointed out in this passage—this allegorical story of the signature is not without its own "Lazarus, arise!"—its resurrection, and above all its "ghost" story.

. . . The final closing of the form, constantly postponed, occurs so swiftly and suddenly that *it hides its dependence on previous moments* (my italics) in its own precipitous instantaneity. The entire process tries to outrun time, to achieve a swiftness that would transcend the latent opposition between action and form.

In M[onsieur] G[uys]'s manner, two features can be observed; in the first place, the contention of a highly suggestive, resurrecting power of memory, a memory that addresses all things with: "Lazarus, arise!"; on the other hand, a fiery, intoxicating vigor of pencil and brushstroke that almost resembles fury. He seems to be in anguish of not going fast enough, of letting the phantom escape before the synthesis has been extracted from it and been recorded. . . . you may call this a sketch if you like, but it is a perfect sketch.

That Baudelaire has to refer to this synthesis as a "phantom" is another instance of the rigor that forces him to double any assertion by a qualifying use of language that puts it at once into question. The Constantin Guys of the essay is himself a *phantom, bearing some resemblance to the actual painter, but differing from him in being the fictional achievement* of what existed only potentially in the "real" man. Even if we consider the character in the essay to be a mediator used to formulate the *prospective vision* of Baudelaire's own work, we can still witness in this vision a similar *disincarnation and reduction of meaning.* (p. 158, my italics)

Let me recall that the quotation from Baudelaire and his discourse on the phantom comes from a text entitled "Mnemonic Art." At the very beginning of *Le Peintre de la vie moderne,* the work to which "Mnemonic Art" belongs, the phantom makes its first appearance— as the very attraction or provocativeness of the past: "Le passé, tout en gardant le piquant du fantôme, reprendra la lumière et le mouvement de la vie, et se fera présent." ("Without losing anything of its ghostly piquancy, the past will recover the light and movement of life and will become present.")

Ghosts always pass quickly, with the infinite speed of a furtive apparition, in an instant without duration, presence without present of a present which, coming back, only *haunts.* The ghost, *le re-venant,* the survivor, appears only by means of figure or fiction, but its appearance is not nothing, nor is it a mere semblance. And this "synthesis as a phantom" enables us to recognize in the figure of the phantom the working of what Kant and Heidegger assign to the transcendental imagination and whose temporalizing schemes and power of synthesis are indeed "fantastic"—are, in Kant's phrase, those of an *art hidden* in the depths of the soul.

There is the art of memory and there is the memory of art.

Art is a thing of the past; remember Hegel's provocative declaration. Paul de Man offers an equally provocative reading of it in his essay on "Sign and Symbol in Hegel's *Aesthetics.*" We now return to it after this detour, but in fact the interpretive debate with the Hegelian dialectic has not been interrupted. The theme of the fantastic and of the arts of "productive memory" is common, moreover, despite many differences, both to Kant and to Hegel. It is intrinsically a question of an art *and* of the origin of the arts, the productive source of symbols and signs.

Since he emphasizes the (non-dialectical) break between *Gedächtnis* and *Erinnerung,* Paul de Man rein-terprets the famous adage, "art is a thing of the past." In the last three pages of his essay, the first moment of his displacement seems to me characteristic of a certain style of "deconstructive" reading. The second moment, at the very end of his text, is an analogous operation, this time on the subject of allegory. Between these two moments, Proust serves as a mediating phantom and symbolic example.

In this way we are slowly, carefully, timidly ap-proaching a question concerning so-called "decon-struction in America." One will not understand it all, but certainly one will understand nothing at all of it, if one does not attempt to decipher the ways it has been marked or signed by de Man's idiom, by the singularity of his stamp.

If art is a thing of the past, this comes from its link, through writing, the sign, *technè,* with that think-ing memory, that memory without memory, with that power of *Gedächtnis* without *Erinnerung.* This power, we now know, is *pre-occupied* by a past which has never been present and will never allow itself to be reani-mated in the interiority of consciousness.

We are quite close here to a thinking memory (*Gedächtnis*) whose movement carries an essential affir-mation, a kind of engagement beyond negativity, that is to say also beyond the bereaved interiority of symbolist introjection (*Erinnerung*): a thinking memory of fidel-ity, a reaffirmation of engagement, but a memory that has done its mourning for the dialectic (which is mourning itself); and consequently memory without mourning, the rigorous fidelity of an affirmation that cannot be called an "amnesic" except in relation to the symbolic appropriation of interior recollection. We must think at the same time the two sources: Mnemosyne, Lethe. Translate this, if you like, as: we must keep in memory the difference of Lethe from Mnemosyne, which we may call *aletheia*.

Yesterday I asked where to look for, and how to locate, the sort of affirmative thought that I have always sensed and appreciated in and beyond the most critical and "ironical" moments of Paul de Man's work. We find ourselves here in its vicinity.

Does not the most affirmative fidelity, its most concerned *act* of memory, involve us with an absolute past, not reducible to any form of presence: the dead being that will never itself return, never again be there, present to answer to or to share this faith? Some would immediately conclude that with the economy of interiorization, mourning, and dialectic, with this *fidelity to self*, Narcissus, who turns back to himself, has returned. No doubt this is true, but what of that if the self (*soi-même*) has that relation to itself only *through* the other, through the promise (for the future, as trace of the future) made to the other as an absolute past, and thus *through* this absolute past, thanks to the other whose sur-vival—that is, whose mortality—always exceeded the "we" of a common present? In the present instant, the "living present" which brings together two friends—and this is friendship—this incredible scene of memory is written in the absolute past; it dictates the madness of an amnesic fidelity, of a forgetful hypermnesia, the gravest and yet the lightest.

Of the two springs called Mnemosyne and Lethe, which is the right one for Narcissus? The other.

Art is a thing of the past because its memory is without memory; one cannot *recover* this past—as soon as the work comes into being—since the memory

Erinnerung) of it is refused. The whole argument of the essay tends toward this conclusion: there is no *dialectical* passage from the symbol to the sign. Art, like thought or thinking memory, is linked to the sign and not the symbol. It thus has dealings only with the absolute past—that is, the immemorial or unrememberable, with an archive that no interiorizing memory can take into itself.

To the extent that the paradigm for art is thought rather than perception, the sign rather than the symbol, writing rather than painting or music, it will also be memorization rather than recollection. As such, it belongs indeed to a past which, in Proust's words, could never be recaptured, *retrouvé*. Art is "of the past" in a radical sense, in that, like memorization, it leaves the interiorization of experience forever behind. (p. 773)

The next sentence alludes once again to that materiality which I earlier emphasized is neither "metaphysical" nor "dialectizable": "It is of the past to the extent that it *materially* inscribes, and thus forever forgets, its ideal content."

It goes without saying—and thus I won't dwell on it—that this interpretation of the letter in Hegel, of its material inscription, is, precisely, strong thinking, taking a risk. It is easy to see what sort of reading of Hegel or theory of reading Hegel could lead one to set against it a quite different perspective. This has been done (Raymond Geuss, "A Response to Paul de Man," *Critical Inquiry* [December 1983] vol. 10), and it could be done in yet another way. But what concerns me here is what this strong interpretation challenges or displaces in the system of traditional, philological assumptions, in the normative theory of reading (that of Hegel in particular)

that is presupposed by both philosophical institutions
and literary institutions, but also by the academic debates that sometimes oppose them to one another. Paul
de Man shows this in his "Reply to Raymond Geuss,"
and I refer you to these few pages. They tell us more
about the institutions and strategies of reading, about
their implications and political effects, about their som-
nolence as well, their amnesia, than all the pious reci-
tations or bits of revolutionary bravura, which only
revolve in place. Here are just a few lines of this answer,
to move us toward the question of a "deconstructive"
strategy:

What is suggested by a reading such as the one I propose is
that difficulties and discontinuities (rather than "vacilla-
tions," which is Geuss' term rather than mine) remain in
even as masterful and tight a text as the *Aesthetics*. These
difficulties have left their mark or have even shaped the history of the understanding of Hegel up to the present. They
cannot be resolved by the canonical system explicitly established by Hegel himself, namely, the dialectic. This is why
these difficulties have at all times been used as a point of
entry into the critical examination of the dialectic as such.
In order to account for them, it is indispensable that one
not only listen to what Hegel openly, officially, literally,and
canonically asserts but also to what is being said obliquely,
figurally, and implicitly (though not less compellingly) in
less conspicuous parts of the corpus. Such a way of reading
is by no means willful; it has its own constraints, perhaps
more demanding than those of canonization. (*Critical Inquiry*
[December 1983] 10(2):389-390)

Such a strategy thus leads one to recognize and
to analyze in Hegel's *Aesthetics* the strange corpus of a
text whose unity and homogeneity are not guaranteed
by the reassuring singleness of a meaning: a "double
and possibly duplicitous text" which *intends* "the pres-

THE ART OF MEMOIRES

ervation and the monumentalization of classical art" yet
which *happens to describe* "all the elements which make
such a preservation impossible from the start."

This move induces another. Between the two, to
move from one to the other, a quotation from Proust
explains that a symbol is not represented symbolically,
"non comme un symbole, puisque la pensée symbolisée
n'[est] pas representée, mais comme réel, comme effec-
tivement subi or *materiellement* manié" (not as a symbol,
since the symbolized thought is not expressed, but as
real, as actually experienced or materially handled).
(For the same reasons as before, I italicize the word
materially in Proust's sentence.) This sentence comes
from a passage of *Du Côté de chez Swann* which speaks of
allegory in Giotto's frescoes. But once again, what is
allegory? Hegel discusses it in passages which concern
forms of art that are neither beautiful nor aesthetic. It is
not by chance that these are the same passages in
which, as de Man writes, "the theory of the sign manifests itself *materially*" (my italics). Allegory is "ugly"
(*kahl*); it belongs to late symbolic modes, to the self-
consciously symbolic modes characteristic of the "inferior genres" (*untergeordnete Gattungen*). But this servile
inferiority, this mechanical instrumentality of the slave,
can become or may have been the place of the master:
just as much in what concerns the concept of allegory *in*
Hegel's text as in what might constitute the allegorical
structure or functioning *of* Hegel's own text. In the following passage I emphasize the *just as* which articulates
the different moments of the analogy:

Before allowing Hegel's dismissal [of allegory] to dismiss the
problem, one should *remember* [I emphasize the irony] that,
in a truly dialectical system such as Hegel's here one recalls
the dialectic to its true self, but in order to make it "beside

itself"], what appears to be inferior and enslaved (*unter-geordnet*) may well turn out to be the master. Compared to the depth and beauty of recollection, memory appears as a mere tool, a mere slave of the intellect, *just as* the sign appears shallow and mechanical compared to the aesthetic *aura* of the symbol, or *just as* prose appears like piecework labor next to the noble craft of poetry—*just as*, we may add, *neglected corners* in the Hegelian canon are perhaps masterful articulations rather than the all too visible synthetic judgments that are being *remembered* [my italics] as the commonplaces of nineteenth-century history. The section on allegory, apparently so conventional and disappointing, may well be a case in point. (pp. 774-75)

I have emphasized "neglected corners" and, twice, the verb "remember": "one should remember" something— the true dialectic—so as to oppose it to what is in fact remembered, "the synthetic judgments that are being remembered," the conventional Hegelianism, perhaps the dialectic itself. The forgotten dialectic must be recalled *against* the dialectic that persists in all memories, especially that of a tradition whose latent Hegelianism dominates the interpretation of English Romanticism. This is a lateral but significant target of the essay (cf. p. 771). One is always playing one memory against another, but here, by a supplementary paradox or chiasmus, Paul de Man *appears to be playing* a supplement of dialectic against the untrue dialectic; he seems to play at reminding us what *must be remembered,* must be recalled to vigilance, called to life, recalled to good memory against bad dozing memory, against the dogmatic slumbers of a tradition. One might recall here the implacable law that always opposes good (living) memory to bad memory (mechanical, technical, on the side of death): Plato's *anamnesis* or *mneme* to *hypomneme*, the good to the bad *pharmakon*. But on the one hand, Paul de Man is manifestly playing when he invokes the "true" dialectic; and, on the other hand, by a reversal which ought in fact to displace the structure, what he ultimately wants us to recall is not the good-living-memory but on the contrary the essential mutual implication of thought and of what the tradition defines as "bad" memory, the technique of memory, writing, the abstract sign, and—in the same series—the figure of allegory. It is thus to the power of *forgetting* that his "one should remember" recalls us, to what the till-now dominant interpretation calls *forgetting* because it takes true memory to be that of "recollection" in the supposedly living interiority of the soul, *Erinnerung*.

We are here called to recall what we must *think:* thought is not bereaved interiorization; it thinks at boundaries, it thinks the boundary, the limit of interiority. And to do this is also to think the art of memory, as well as the memory of art. One more step before closing this parenthesis: these two memories are doubtless not *opposed* to one another; they are not two. And if this unity, this contamination or contagion is not dialectical, perhaps we should recall (recall ourselves to) a memory already "older" than *Gedächtnis* and *Erinnerung*. To what law and what memory of the law, to what law of memory would this "we should" then recall us?

In very traditional fashion Hegel makes the purpose of allegory pedagogical and expository. It must be clear, and personification is thought to have this expository virtue. But the subject, the "I" of allegory, must remain abstract, general, almost "grammatical." Yet the qualities of the allegorized abstraction (think of Truth or Memory, Vice or Virtue, Life or Death, Memory or

Oblivion) must be recognizable (*erkennbar*), says Hegel, and thus beyond the abstract grammaticality of the "I". Here we come back to the reading of "Was ich nur meine, ist mein" (paragraph 20 of the *Encyclopedia*) and the self-effacement of the *I* which eclipses itself "just as" "memory effaces remembrance (or recollection)" (p. 773):

What the allegory narrates is, therefore, in Hegel's own words, "the separation or disarticulation of subject from predicate *(die Trennung von Subjekt und Prädikat)."* For discourse to be meaningful, this separation has to take place, yet it is incompatible with the necessary generality of all meaning. Allegory functions, categorically and logically, like the *defective cornerstone* of the entire system. (p. 775, my italics)

We have here a figure of what some might be tempted to see as the dominant metaphorical register, indeed the allegorical bent of "deconstruction," a certain architectural rhetoric. One first locates, in an architechtonics, in the art of the system, the "neglected corners" and the *"defective* cornerstone," that which, from the outset, threatens the coherence and the internal order of the construction. But it is a cornerstone! It is required by the architecture which it nevertheless, in advance, deconstructs from within. It assures its cohesion while situating in advance, in a way that is both visible and invisible (that is, corner), the site that lends itself to a deconstruction to come. The best spot for efficiently inserting the deconstructive lever is a cornerstone. There may be other analogous places but this one derives its privilege from the fact that it is indispensable to the completeness of the edifice. A condition of erection, holding up the walls of an established edifice, it also can be said to maintain it, to contain it, and to be tantamount to the *generality* of the architectonic system, "of the entire system."

Paul de Man's "deconstructive" moves do not all obey this logic or this "architectural" rhetoric. Nor do I think, but I will explain this elsewhere, that deconstruction—if there be such a thing and it be *one*—is bound by the link that the word suggests with the architectonic. Rather, it attacks the systemic (i.e., architectonic) constructionist account of what is brought together, of assembly. Before returning to the strange equivalence of the part to the whole, of the cornerstone to the generality of the system, let me just mark here, with a stepping-stone, perhaps, the location of a problem—of non-architectonic *Versammlung*—which I shall attempt to develop elsewhere.

As we have seen, the very condition of a deconstruction may be at work, in the work, *within* the system to be deconstructed; it may *already* be located there, already at work, not at the center but in an excentric center, in a corner whose eccentricity assures the solid concentration of the system, participating in the construction of what it at the same time threatens to deconstruct. One might then be inclined to reach this conclusion: deconstruction is not an operation that supervenes *afterwards,* from the outside, one fine day; it is always already at work in the work; one must just know how to identify the right or wrong element, the right or wrong stone—the right one, of course, always proves to be, precisely, the wrong one. Since the disruptive force of deconstruction is always already contained within the architecture of the work, all one would finally have to do to be able to deconstruct, given this *always already,* is to do memory work. Since I want neither to accept or to reject a conclusion formulated in these terms, let us leave this question hanging for a while.

If allegory is "the defective cornerstone of the entire system," it is also a figure for its most effective cornerstone. As a cornerstone, it supports it, however rickety it may be, and brings together at a single point all its forces and tensions. It does not do this from a central commanding point, like a *keystone*; but it also does it, laterally, in its corner. It represents the whole in a point and at every instant; it centers it, as it were, in a periphery, shapes it, stands for it. Since in this case the cornerstone is the concept of allegory, one can legitimately conclude that allegory, this part of aesthetics, has the rhetorical value of a metonymy or a synecdoche (part for the whole). And since the concept of allegory (as a metonymy) means something other than what it says through a figure about the system, it constitutes a kind of allegorical trope in the most general sense of the term. If allegory is an allegory (a condition which, let us note in passing, can never by definition be definitively assured), if the prescribed concept of allegory is an allegory of the Hegelian system, then the entire functioning of the system becomes allegorical. To radicalize by accelerating this matter, one could say that the entire Hegelian dialectic is a vast allegory. Paul de Man does not put it in this way, but he sees in Hegelianism a specific allegory; not, as is often believed, the allegory of synthesizing and reconciliatory power, but that of disjunction, dissociation, and discontinuity. It is the power of allegory, and its ironic force as well, to say something quite different from and even contrary to what seems to be intended through it. And since this allegory is what made possible, before and after Hegel, the construction of even the concept of history, philosophy of history and history of philosophy, one should no longer rely on something like history (in the philosophical sense of the word "history") to account for this "allegoricity." The usual concept of history is itself one of its effects; it bears its mark and stamp (*estampille*).

Thenceforth the disjunction (*Trennung von Subjekt und Prädikat*) which divides the allegorical structure of allegory reproduces itself without check. This is Paul de Man's conclusion, and his diagnosis is not historical throughout; it is also presented as a diagnosis *of* a certain concept of history and of the *limits* of a certain historicism:

We would have to conclude that Hegel's philosophy which, like his *Aesthetics,* is a philosophy of history (and of aesthetics) as well as a history of philosophy (and of aesthetics)—and the Hegelian corpus indeed contains texts that bear these two symmetrical titles—is *in fact* [I emphasize this expression which bears all the weight of this de- or re-construction] an allegory of the disjunction between philosophy and history, or, in our more restricted concern, between literature and aesthetics, or, more narrowly still, between literary experience and literary theory. The reasons for this disjunction, which it is equally vain to deplore or to praise, are not themselves historical or recoverable by way of history. To the extent that they are inherent in language, in the *necessity, which is also an impossibility* [my italics], to connect the subject with its predicates or the sign with its symbolic significations, the disjunction will always, as it did in Hegel, manifest itself as soon as experience shades into thought, history into theory. No wonder that literary theory has such a bad name, all the more so since the emergence of thought and of theory is not something that our own thought can hope to prevent or to control. (p. 775)

Hegel's philosophy, reread from the most deficient and efficient cornerstone, is said to be—over its dead body—an allegory of disjunction. Over its dead body, in a kind of essential denegation, able to ventriloquize the entire dialectic, the "true" as well as the other; but it would be an allegory of disjunction through and through, over its entire body. But what can an allegory of disjunction signify when the structure of allegory it-self has as its essential *trait* this *dis-traction* from self that is disjunction? After "The Rhetoric of Temporality"[4] Paul de Man never ceased to insist on allegorical dis-junction and the history of its interpretation (Goethe, Schiller, Coleridge, and so forth). If allegory is disjunc-tive, an allegory of disjunction will always remain a disjoined reflexivity, an allegory of allegory that can never, in its specular self-reflection, rejoin itself, fit itself to itself. Its memory will promise but never provide a chance for re-collecting itself, for the *Versammlung* in which a thinking of being could collect itself.

Let us leave this thread trailing in the labyrinth. Its law will later make us double back on our tracks and once again cross those of Hölderlin and Heidegger. This labyrinth not only borders on the two sources, Mnemosyne and Lethe; it takes the form of a path which leads us back and forth from one to the other.

The disjunctive structure of allegory, as an alle-gory of allegory, compels us to complicate the schema I sketched earlier, and for this I must review the distinc-tion between a keystone and a cornerstone. If the defec-tive cornerstone of allegory has a certain relation to the cohesion of "the entire system," as de Man puts it, and if it is thereby the allegory of a system itself allegorical, it nevertheless cannot *count for* the whole. It is not placed in the center and at the apex of a totality whose forces all join at one point, the keystone—which in this case would be the sole key to interpretation, the major signified or the signifier for a reading. This is why Paul de Man does not say that the "defective cornerstone of the entire system" *counts for the whole*. In "The Rhetoric of Temporality" emphasis falls not just on the narrative structure of allegory but primarily on its disjunctive

structure. Consequently an allegory can never be reduced to a metaphor, to a symbol, nor even to a metonymy or a synecdoche which would designate "the
totality of which they are a part" (p. 190). This disjunctive, de-totalizing quality no doubt explains why de
Man never ceases to privilege the figure of allegory, setting it always against the tradition of the symbol, be it
German or Anglo-American, in the domain of philosophy, literature, or literary theory, particularly that
which in the United States has developed around Romanticism. One cannot understand this privileging of
allegory—I was long puzzled by it for this very reason—
if one is not familiar with the internal debates of Anglo-
American criticism concerning Romanticism. The tour
de force and special contribution of Paul de Man comes,
no doubt, from his success in making the disturbing
graft of a German tradition on an Anglo-American tradition. The novelty was not the graft itself but the inci-
sions it required here and there. It was necessary, here
and there, to cut short or cut off, to bring out the cut
separating allegory from other figures. This explains his
interest in Schlegel and Benjamin, in opposition, on
this point, to a tradition running from Goethe to
Gadamer.[5]

   If Hegel's philosophy represents an allegory of
disjunction, an allegory of allegories, one must conclude that it cannot itself be totalized by an interpretation, and above all that it is not a figure for anamnesic
totalization, a great gathering together of all the figures
of Western metaphysics, its completion and its limit, as
it is often thought to be—whatever conclusions one
then draws. And if the Hegelian concept of allegory,
"like the defective cornerstone of the entire system" (an
expression in which one must hear a certain irony, as

we did earlier in "truly dialectical system"), says something about the "whole" Hegelian text, what it says,
while remaining in its limited, partial, circumscribed
place, which could not symbolize the "whole," is that
there is no "entire system": the whole is not totalized;
the system is constructed with the aid of a defective
cornerstone, despite or thanks to this stone which deconstructs it. The essential point of support this lateral
stone provides is no more a foundation than a keystone.
It is, and it says, the other; it is an allegory.

Hence allegory, despite a privileging one might
judge exorbitant, still remains one figure among others.
One could certainly play a game of substitution which
would mobilize all the turns of rhetoric: allegory as the
privileged figure would become the allegory of all the
other figures. It would fill the role of metonymy or
synecdoche, a part for the whole, or that of metaphor,
etc., so that each of these figures could,in turn, take the
place of allegory—each becoming the metaphor or
metonymy of all the others, since the self-reflexivity of
this process has no end. But in fact, it seems to me that
for de Man allegory is only quasi-privileged: it is not
simply what it assuredly is as well, a rhetorical figure.
Nor is rhetoric simply rhetoric, if by that one means a
determinable, "terminable" genealogy that gives rise to
a masterable catalogue of technical possibilities. And
yet, for good reasons, de Man does not wish to further
efface or submerge these particularizing, restricting limits. To do this would be to revert to a transcendentaliz-
ing and homogenizing totalization (on the model of
metaphor or symbol).

Now if allegory *remains* a figure, and one figure
among others, at the very moment when, articulating
the limit, it marks an excess, it is because it says in

another way something *about the other*. If one could es-
tablish an opposition (which I do not believe) or differ-
entiate (something else again), one might say that
between memory of being and memory of the other
there is perhaps the disjunction of allegory. But let us
not forget that a disjunction does not only separate,
whether we are dealing with the Hegelian concept of
allegory, the allegory of disjunction, or allegory *as*
disjunction. Even if it is defective, the cornerstone supports and joins, holds together what it separates. We
will come back later to the memory of being and the
memory of the other. What these words say is no doubt
not the same thing, but perhaps they speak of the same
thing.

　　　Since I have just alluded to Heidegger, of whom
we will speak tomorrow, let me recall once more the
passage in "Heidegger's Exegeses of Hölderlin" where
Paul de Man resolutely determines, draws a line, even
italicizing to sharpen the decisiveness of the distinction:
"There is, however, another much deeper reason that
justifies this choice: *it is the fact that Hölderlin says exactly
the opposite of what Heidegger makes him say.*" He then
continues:

Such an assertion is paradoxical only in appearance. At this
level of thought it is difficult to distinguish between a proposition and that which constitutes its opposite. In fact, to state
the opposite is still to talk of the same thing though in an
opposite sense, and it is already a major achievement to have,
in a dialogue of this sort, the two interlocutors manage to
speak of the same thing. (It can be said that Heidegger and
Hölderlin speak of the same thing.) (*Blindness and Insight*,
p. 255)

What is "the same thing"? What if "the same thing",

here, were the other? Is there a difference between Being and the other?

The "same thing," under consideration since yesterday, we have called "memory." Is this an appropriate noun, a proper name, a unique name? We recalled ourselves to the name Mnemosyne, and we recalled, in the name of Mnemosyne, that *one must not forget Lethe,* that is the truth (aletheia).

With the name Mnemosyne, do Hölderlin, Heidegger, and de Man say the same thing? Surely not. But do they speak of the same thing? Perhaps. This question will be raised again tomorrow. But it will never leave us; it will haunt us like the phantoms of all the prosopopoeias or parabases which, in de Man's later writing, have been brought in simply to take up the idea of allegory, even irony.

All these figures, remember, are also ghostly figures. As we read in Baudelaire, they speak like phantoms in the text, certainly, but above all they phantomize the text itself. It remains to be seen what the phantom means or—this can have still other meanings—what the word phantom, the word "phantom," the *"word"* phantom means. In a phantom-text, these distinctions, these quotation marks, references, or citations become irremediably precarious; they leave only traces, and we shall never define the trace or the phantom without, ironically or allegorically, appealing from one to the other.

Is it by chance that, in the very first steps by which he reopened the problem of allegory, Paul de Man convoked the ghost of Coleridge, and the phantom of which Coleridge speaks, precisely in relation to allegory? Allegory speaks (through) the voice of the other, whence the ghost-effect, whence also the a-symbolic disjunction:

Its structure [the symbol's] is that of the synecdoche, for the symbol is always part of the totality it represents. Consequently, in the symbolical imagination, no disjunction of the constitutive faculties takes place, since the material perception and the symbolical imagination are continuous, as this part is continuous with the whole. In contrast, the allegorical form appears purely mechanical, an abstraction whose original meaning is even more devoid of substance than its "phantom proxy," the allegorical representative; it is an immaterial shape that represents a sheer phantom devoid of shape and substance. (*Blindness and Insight,* p. 191-92. The quotation is from Coleridge, *The Statesman's Manual.*)

But should we disjoin this ghostly disjunction called allegory from that other ghostly disjunction called irony? As the following example shows, Paul de Man insists on both moves at once: to bring out the distinctiveness of allegory, a particular figure whose particularity does not have metonymical or synecdochic value, but simultaneously to grant it the right of communication (if not non-symbolic, nontotalizing participation) with other figures, perhaps with all the others, not, precisely, by resemblance, through the voice or way of the *same,* but by the voice or way of the *other,* of difference and disjunction. Paul de Man is bent on demonstrating "the implicit and rather enigmatic link" (p. 208) for allegory and irony; we have already glimpsed it for synecdoche, prosopopoeia, or parabasis. Irony too is a figure of disjunction, duplication, and doubling (pp. 212, 217, etc.). It often produces a disjunction by which "a purely linguistic subject replaces the original self" (p. 217), according to the scheme of amnesic memory of which we have spoken. And yet, precisely because of the disjunctive structure that they share, allegory and irony draw up between them this singular contract, and each recalls the other. Of course, the former is essentially narrative, the latter momentary and pointed (*instantaneiste*), but together they form, in fact, the rhetoric of memory which recalls, recounts, forgets, recounts, and recalls forgetting, referring to the past only to efface what is essential to it: anteriority. At the beginning of this lecture I quoted a passage describing the modernity of Baudelaire or Nietzsche as "a forgetting or a suppression of anteriority." Now here, at the moment where the rhetoric of temporality finally brings together allegory and irony, after having separated them, we find the "same" structure, the most profound and the least profound: "an unreachable anteriority."

Our description seems to have reached a provisional conclusion. The act of irony . . . reveals the existence of a temporality that is definitely not organic. . . . Irony divides the flow of temporal experience into a past that is a pure mystification and a future that remains harassed forever by a relapse within the inauthentic. It can know this inauthenticity but can never overcome it . . . . It dissolves in the narrowing spiral of a linguistic sign that becomes more and more remote from its meaning, and it can find no escape from this spiral. The temporal void that it reveals is the same void we encountered when we found allegory always implying an unreachable anteriority. Allegory and irony are thus linked in their common discovery of a truly temporal predicament. They are also linked in their common demystification of an organic world postulated in a symbolic mode of analogical correspondences or in a mimetic mode of representation in which fiction and reality could coincide.

Then, beyond this provisional conclusion, here is the *link* between these two figures of memory: the one pretends to know how to tell stories—this is diachronic allegory—and the other feigns amnesia—this is synchronic allegory. But neither has a past anterior:

Essentially the mode of the present, it [irony] knows neither memory nor prefigurative duration, whereas allegory exists entirely within an ideal time that is never here and now but always a past or an endless future. Irony is a synchronic structure, while allegory appears as a successive mode capable of engendering duration as the illusion of a continuity that it knows to be illusionary. Yet the two modes, for all their profound distinction in mood and structure, are the two faces of the *same fundamental experience of time.* . . . Both modes are fully de-mystified when they remain within the realm of their respective languages but are totally vulnerable to renewed blindness as soon as they leave it for the empirical world. Both are determined by an *authentic experience of temporality* which, seen from the point of view of the self engaged in the world, is a negative one. The dialectical play between the two modes as well as their common interplay with mystified forms of language (such as symbolic or mimetic representation), which it is not in their power to eradicate, make up what is called literary history. (p. 226. My italics)

If, in concluding today, I underline several of the questions that these relatively early texts of Paul de Man address to us or pose for us, it is not because I find these texts old or problematical. On the contrary, I think I have brought them into resonance with the most recent. Nor is it by some rhetorical feint, as if I were holding back expressible answers to these questions, making you wait for them until at least tomorrow. No, tomorrow we shall doubtless encounter these questions, again in one form or another, but they will still remain open. What are they?

1. Is there a relation and, if so, what, between "the dialectical play of the two [rhetorical] modes," or this discourse on mystification, demystification, and "the authentic experience of temporality," on the one hand, and something like "deconstruction" on the

other—if there be such a thing and it be *one*—whether
in the writings of Paul de Man or of others? And what
relation is there between Paul de Man's and any other? I
say "deconstruction" and not the problematic of deconstruction, as is sometimes said, nor deconstructive
criticism, for deconstruction is not—for reasons that are
essential—problematic; it is not a problematic (a brief
deconstructive history of the word *problem* would
quickly show this, as one for the word *criticism* would
show that there cannot be a deconstructive criticism,
since deconstruction is more or less, or in any case other
than a criticism).

    2. If one can join together in the "same" experi-
ence of time these two disjunctive forces of allegory and
irony, does that promise us an anamnesis which goes
back "further" than these two opposing sources (the
allegorical Mnemosyne and the ironic Lethe which
"knows neither memory nor prefigurative duration")?
Would there be a "more ancient" figure, a more originary, more "fundamental" experience of time than that of
this rhetorical disjunction? Would this figure still be,
would it still have a figure, or would it remain "prefig-
ural?" Is there a memory for this prefiguration? Is not
this text of Paul de Man's moving toward (or, rather,
moving *as*) this more ancient but still newer memory,
turned like a promise toward the future? Is not *that* his
practice, his style, his signature, the stamp of his deconstruction? I speak of the signature because this entire series of questions thrusts itself upon me at the
moment where there appears a kind of hybrid of two
memories, or of a memory and an amnesia which di-
vide the same act. As if the ironic moment were signed,
were sealed in the body of an allegorical writing.

    A page further on Paul de Man speaks of a novelist who manages to be at the same time an allegorist and an ironist. He would, in brief, know how to tell a story, but he would refrain from doing so, without one ever being able to know whether he were telling the truth. Such a novelist, says Paul de Man, "has to seal, so to speak, the ironic moments within the allegorical duration" (p. 227). "Irony of ironies"—thus would be stamped the permanent parabases of Paul de Man's Schlegel, for example.

3. Even if this memory of prefiguration were possible, we know that it would offer no "anteriority" that was not fictive or figural; it could only "suppress" or "forget" it. What follows?

4. Would a radical memory without anteriority, an anamnesis which would radically dispense with an anterior past, still be an experience of temporality? Do its figures belong to a rhetoric of temporality or a rhetoric of spacing? Is not rhetoric or figuration as an art of memory always an art of space? For what has no past anterior would swiftly be seen by some as nothing less than space. It cannot be as simple as that, but the interpretation of the essential relation between *Gedächtnis* (thinking memory *and* technical memory or act of writing) and spatial recording, the exteriority of the sign, etc. marks a kind of spacing, a gap that is not contradiction, between "The Rhetoric of Temporality" (1969) and "Sign and Symbol . . . " (1982).

5. What does a memory without anteriority recall, what does it promise? Is it a memory without origin, genealogy, history or filiation? Must one at each instant *reinvent* filiation? Some would see here the signature of a faithful memory, even its affirmation; others would denounce in it a concealment or betrayal, and dismiss it as a figure of the simulacrum.

Yesterday, you may remember, I began by telling you that I suffer from an inability to tell a story, without knowing whether I suffer from amnesia or hypermnesia. It is because I cannot tell a story that I turn to myth. But Mnemosyne, Lethe, Atropos or her two sisters are not only myths; they are also allegories in the strict sense, personifications of Memory, Forgetting, Death; and they are always family romances, stories of filiation, of sons and daughters. Mnemosyne, the mother of the muses, was also the wife of Zeus, with whom she was united for nine years. Do not forget the Moirai; Atropos, Clotho, and Lachesis, those who spin and cut the thread of life, are also daughters of Zeus— and of Themis. But I should also remind you of the character Mnemon: he who remembers but above all makes one remember. He is an auxiliary, a technician, an artist of memory, a remembering or hypomnesic servant. Achilles, whom he served, received him from his mother on the eve of the Trojan War. Mnemon had an unusual mission: an agent of memory, like an external memory, he was to remind Achilles of an oracle. This oracle had predicted that if Achilles killed a son of Apollo, he would die at Troy. Mnemon was therefore supposed to remind Achilles of the genealogy of anyone whom he was about to kill: Remember, you mustn't kill the son of Apollo. Remember the oracle. Now one day, at Tenedos, Achilles killed Tenes, the son of Apollo. He thus hastened toward the death to which he was destined, through this error or failure of memory, through this lapse of Mnemon. But before dying, in order to punish him, Achilles killed Mnemon with a single blow, with the point of his spear.

Notes

1. Cf. Austin, *How to Do Things with Words*, Sixth Lecture, pp. 67–68.

2. This *inexistence* of the past or of death, in other words their *literal* non-presence, is also their fictive or figural value. It does not reduce mourning (before or after death) to the futility of an illusion. "Allegory," in this case, does not signify, at least in their traditional or usual meanings, the *imaginary, fantasm, simulacrum,* still less *error.* Allegory is not light and superficial, but it does not belong to a space in which one could calmly apprehend a simple *depth.* Since I do not know from whom I would now ask permission, of whom to ask pardon for such an indiscretion, if not the memory of Paul de Man within myself, I shall take the liberty of quoting, because I also feel an obligation to do so, the last letter I received from Paul de Man. Here, at least, are a few lines: "Tout cela, comme je vous le disais [on the telephone several days before] me semble prodigeusement intéressant et je m'amuse beaucoup. Je l'ai toujours su, mais cela se confirme: la mort gagne beaucoup, comme on dit, à être connue de plus près—ce 'peu profond ruisseau calomnié la mort.'" ["All this, as I was saying to you, seems exceedingly interesting to me, and I am greatly intrigued by it. I always knew it, but it proves to be so: Death repays, as they say, closer acquaintance—'this shallow calumniated stream called death.'"] This is the final line of Mallarmé's "Tomb of Verlaine." Yes, the tomb of Verlaine of Mallarmé, as if, as we have said, the signatory of the epitaph always writes on his own tomb: the tomb of Verlaine of Mallarmé of Paul de Man, etc. This genealogy of genitives cannot be broken by a cenotaph, or by cremation. After citing Mallarmé, Paul de Man adds, "J'aime quand même mieux cela que la brutalité du mot 'tumeur.'" (I certainly prefer that to the brutality of the word "tumeur.")

This letter was already "in memory," it was read in advance as what was *already reread after* the death of him who heard in this way the French word "tumeur," who heard it as a *verdict,* the future soon to follow the sentence, the terrible apostrophe and the "brutality" of familiar address: (*tu meurs*: you are dying, you must die, you shall die.) But the order prescribing the future in the grammar of the present is already a description of a present, the calm statement, "tu meurs": since you must die, already you are dying; I see you and I make you die.

And *already* you are *in memory of* your own death; and your friends as well, and all the others, both of your own death and already of their own through yours. And from all these possible sentences nothing collects on the plane of a single surface or in the unity of some depth. It is "peu profond." Let us not speak ill of death, not speak badly or unjustly of death. Let us not calumniate it; let us learn not to do so. We would run the risk of wounding, in our memory, those whom it bears.

Tumeur: the *act* as inscription in the memory of an older trace, more immemorial than the opposition between some performative act of the order given (*tu meurs,* I order you to die), and the statement of fact which takes cognizance (indeed, *tu meurs,* you are dying; I see it). A question of language and idiom, a memory untranslatable from the French, the word "tumeur" speaks in this way only to francophones. Paul de Man was one, and he wrote this to me in French.

3. And yet reading must find its rhythm, the right measure and just cadence. In the measure, at least, that it attempts to bring us to grasp a meaning that does not come through understanding. Let us recall the epigraph to *Allegories of Reading*: "Quand on lit trop vite ou trop doucement on n'entend rien.' Pascal." (When one reads too swiftly or too slowly one understands nothing.) One should never forget the authoritative ellipsis of this warning. But at what speed ought one to have read it? On the very threshold of the book, it might be swiftly overlooked.

4. Reprinted in *Blindness and Insight* (Univ. of Minnesota Press, 1983), (2d edition).

5. On all these questions (deconstruction, deconstruction and rhetoric, deconstruction and the American tradition) see, of course, Jonathan Culler's fundamental *On Deconstruction: Theory and Criticism After Structuralism* (Cornell University Press, 1982). On the point discussed above, see in particular pp. 185 and 247 ff. Culler cites here a sentence of Paul de Man's which I think describes very well what one might call the "defective cornerstone" effect: "A deconstruction always has for its target to reveal the existence of hidden articulations and fragmentations within assumedly monadic totalities" (*Allegories of Reading*, p. 249). What is at issue here is nothing less than the concept of "nature" in Rousseau: "nature turns out to be a self-deconstructive term." But since allegory works or divides the self's relation to itself, since it plays while working it, as a "defective cornerstone" always does, one might conclude that the very term "self-deconstruction" is another allegory. Let me recall that in French one says of an element or stone that introduces a process of dislocation into an organic whole that *elle y travaille* or that *elle y joue.* The two words are not synonymous in this case, but they both describe a dis-junctive force.

III

ACTS
The meaning of a
given word

Translated by Eduardo Cadava

I announced, as you will perhaps remember, that I would speak of memory.

Parler de mémoire: if a context, as we say, does not remove ambiguity, the expression "parler de mémoire" lends itself in French to phrases whose meaning can differ entirely one from the other. Je parlerai de "mémoire," this can mean that I will speak to you on the subject of what we call memory, on the theme or else on the word "memory." This I have already begun to do without succeeding in rendering this "thing" any simpler, any clearer, any more univocal; which was not, you may suspect, my primary concern. But in my language "je parlerai de mémoire" can mean, and if the context, as we say, lends itself to this, "je parlerai sans note," "I will speak without notes," as if I were able to cite a prior text "by heart," with only the assistance of my memory, here in the sense of *Gedächtnis* or, if you wish, of mnemonics. In the same way, you say "citer de memoire," "to cite from memory," when you no longer even need a Mnemon who would come to whisper your text to you. Here I am not speaking of memory in this last sense, since I am reading what I have written, and if I have written this more than ever with my heart, I do not know my part "by heart."

But what is the heart? In *Was heisst Denken?* (1954), Heidegger meditates upon the mysterious co-appurtenance within which the thought (*Gedachtes*) of thought (*Gedanke*), memory (*Gedächtnis*), devoted thanks (*Dank*) and the heart (*Herz*) are interchanged. He insists upon the value of a recollection or a gathering (*Versammlung*)—something apparently quite different from a dis-junction—which rightly brings together all of these words. And the enigma of this gathering or of this dis-junction will no doubt be our focus (*foyer*) today, the enigma of a subtle and secret *Auseinander-*

setzung between Heidegger and Paul de Man. In order to suggest the tone of this discussion and by way of an exergue, I will begin with two quotations. The first, from Heidegger in *Was heisst Denken?*:

A thought (*Gedachtes*)—where is it, where does it reside? Thought is in need of memory (*Gedächtnis*). Thanks (*Dank*) belongs to thought and its thoughts, to the "*Gedanc.*" But perhaps these assonances of the word "thinking" (*Denken*) in "memory" and "thanks" are superficially and artificially thought up. For in no way do they make apparent what is named by the word "thinking."
   Is thinking a thanking? What does thanking mean here? Does thanks rest in thinking? What does thinking mean here? Is memory no more than a container for the thoughts of thinking or does thinking itself rest in memory? How are thanks and memory related? . . . Let us address our question now to the history of words. It gives us a direction, though the historical representation of this history is still incomplete and will presumably always remain so.
   We hear the hint, echoing in the spoken aspect of the aforementioned words, that the decisive and originally speaking word is: the "*Gedanc.*" But "*Gedanc*" does not mean, when all is said and done, what we currently mean when we today use the word "thought" (*Gedanke*). A thought usually means: an idea, a presentation, an opinion, an inspiration. The originary word "*Gedanc*" says: the gathered (*gesammelte*), all-gathering recollection (*alles versammelnde Gedenken*). "The *Gedanc*" says nearly the same thing as "the soul" (*das Gemüt*), "spirit" (*der muot*), "the heart" (*das Herz*). Thinking, in the sense of this originally speaking word "*Gedanc,*" is almost more original than that thinking of the heart which Pascal, centuries later and already as a countermove against mathematical thinking, attempted to recover.

And much further on: "The '*Gedanc*,' the bottom of the heart, is the gathering together (*versammlung*) of all that concerns us, all that comes to us, all that touches us insofar as we are, as human beings."[1]

I will not analyze this text here: it would require an immense commentary. Let us content ourselves for the moment by underlining the motif of "gathering" (*Versammlung*) or "recollection." To speak to you of "memory," I have often argued, was also to speak of the future. Of the future of a thought, of what Paul de Man has bequeathed to us, but above all, and indissociable from what within this thought of memory thinks the future, of the experience of the coming of the future (*venue de l'à-venir*). And through this, we are not only made a promise, which comes forward and is written as a promise, but it also comes forward and is written as a thought of the promise, probably today the most profound, most singular, and most necessary thought; probably, too, the most difficult and most disconcerting. I do not know if I will today succeed—given the form and the limits of a lecture—in introducing this thought to you, but it is through Paul de Man's texts on the question of the promise (notably through his readings of Rousseau) that I will today struggle to approach it. These texts do not just present themselves as texts *on* the theme of the promise; they demonstrate—show and envelop at the same time—the performative structure of the text in general *as* promise, including that of the demonstrative text, that which Paul de Man signs. This structure never exists without disturbing—I might even say without perverting—the tranquil assurance of the subject of what we today call a "performative." But let us not anticipate too much; we always promise too much. What does it mean to say "promise too much"? A promise is always excessive. Without this essential excess, it would return to a description or knowledge of the future. Its act would have a constative structure and not a performative one. But this "too much" of the promise does not belong to a (promised) content of a promise which I would be incapable of keeping. It is within the very structure of the *act* of promising that this excess comes to inscribe a kind of irremediable disturbance or perversion. This perversion, which is also a trap, no doubt unsettles the language of the promise, the performative as promise; but it also renders it possible—and indestructible. Whence the *unbelievable*, and comical, aspect of every promise, and this passionate attempt to come to terms with the law, the contract, the oath, the declared affirmation of fidelity. At the end of a remarkable demonstration, to which we will return later, Paul de Man writes the following passage—and this will be my second quotation in the form of an exergue (for the moment, I will simply emphasize a few words):

. . . it is impossible to read the *Social Contract* without experiencing the exhilarating feeling inspired by a firm promise, despite the *fact* that its impossibility has been established (the pattern that identifies the *Social Contract* as a *textual* allegory [*textual* is here emphasized by de Man]), does not occur at the discretion of the writer. We are not merely pointing out an inconsistency, a weakness in the text of the *Social Contract* that could have been avoided by simply omitting sentimental or demagogical passages. . . . Even without these passages, the *Social Contract* would still promise by inference, perhaps more effectively than if Rousseau had not had the naïveté, or the good faith, to promise openly. The redoubtable efficacy of the text is due to the rhetorical model of which it is a version. This model is a fact of language over which Rousseau himself has no control [remember here de Man's allusion to the uncontrollable at the end of his text on Hegel]. Just as any other reader, he is bound to misread his text as a promise of politi-

cal change. The error is not within the reader; language itself
dissociates the cognition from the *act*. *Die Sprache verspricht
(sich)*: to the extent that it is *necessarily misleading, language
just as necessarily conveys the promise of its own truth.* This is also
why *textual allegories* on this level of rhetorical complexity
generate history.[2]

   I have at first emphasized the words *"act"* and
"fact": the *act* of language is that of a performative promise whose perverse ambiguity cannot be dominated or
purified, but whose very *act* could not be annulled. A
little before this passage, it had been demonstrated that
the constative and performative functions within certain acts of language ("statements") could neither be
"distinguished" nor "reconciled." This singular aporia,
which divides the act, occurs, if no one can master it, if
we are already committed before any active commitment on our part, and if we are trapped in advance,
because the rhetorical structure of language precedes
the act of our present initiative; it is, if we can say this,
"older." It is a *faktum*, a fact of language which has
established the impossibility of the promise and over
which we have no control. This "fact" is not natural, it is
an artifact, but an artifact which for us—and, primarily,
in this example, for Rousseau—is already there, as a
past which has never been present. We might say that it
is historicity itself—a historicity which cannot be historical, an "ancientness" without history, without anteriority, but which produces history. Before the act, there
is no speech; nor before speech is there an act. There is
this *fact* to which we are recalled by a strange recollection which does not recall any memory.

   In the course of this long exergue, then, I have
placed this fragment from Paul de Man in relation to a
fragment from Heidegger. Later on, I hope or I promise

that the reasons for this will become clearer. For the moment, let us recall that what I have done here again points toward the question of the gathering (*Versammlung*) of Being in its relation or non-relation to law. The day before yesterday, we began with this question, as it arises in Hölderlin, Heidegger, and de Man. We are here in the same place, then, between the promise and memory, thanks and fidelity, thought and the promise of truth ("the promise of its own truth"), probably not far from the heart, and from the heart of the heart. And Paul de Man has just mocked Heidegger a bit. This mockery is already a difference between Paul de Man and Heidegger: Heidegger does not laugh often in his texts; he would probably consider irony as a pose of subjective mastery and he would never have admitted an "exhilarating feeling inspired by a firm promise." Paul de Man smiles, then, and mocks Heidegger a bit by displacing or deforming a citation, by displacing or deforming the celebrated and so misunderstood *Die Sprache spricht*. Speech speaks, language speaks. Many—this is not the case with Paul de Man—have read this phrase with a sneer, as if they were before an empty and intransitive tautology which would have the supplementary weakness of hypostasizing speech (*la parole*), general language (*le langage*) or language (*la langue*). In truth, it is a question, guided by the most necessary movement, of *taking note* (*prendre acte*) of the *fact* that language is not the governable instrument of a speaking being (or subject) and that its essence cannot appear through any other instance than that of the very language which names it, says it, gives it to be thought, speaks it. We cannot even say that language is or does something, nor even that it "acts"; all of these values (being, doing, acting) are insufficient to construct a

ACTS 97

metalanguage on the subject of language. Language speaks *of and by itself,* which is something quite different from a specular tautology. Now what does Paul de Man do here? He takes note of this necessity that *Die Sprache spricht.* He takes it with a certain measure of seriousness. But in miming it, in *its* language, in German, he replaces *spricht* with *verspricht,* "speaks" with "promises." This is another way of saying that the essence of speech is the promise, that there is no speaking that does not promise, which at the same time means a commitment toward the future through what we too hastily call a "speech act" and a commitment to keep the memory of the said act, to keep the acts of this act.

Would Heidegger have judged this transformation of *spricht* into *verspricht* to be inadmissible? We will soon see why the answer to this question is neither so certain, nor so simple. But he would certainly have sketched out the following objection: yes, but in order to promise, it is necessary to speak; in order to think the *versprechen,* the "promise," it is necessary at first to think the *sprechen,* the "speaking"; the *versprechen* is only a modalization—no doubt essential, but peculiar— of the *Sprache.* Now the discreet parody which complicates *spricht* with *verspricht* suggests, on the contrary, that there is no originary and essential *Sprechen* which is then modalized into a promise. Everything begins with this apparently post-originary and performative modalization of *Sprache* [a difficult word to translate simply by language (*langue*), general language (*langage*) or speech (*parole*)]. This is not to say that all of this performativity is of the type of the promise, in the narrow and everyday sense of the term. But this performative thereby reveals a structure or destination of the *Sprache* which compels us to say *Die Sprache verspricht* (*sich*) and no longer sim-

ply *Die Sprache spricht*. But this is not all. Paul de Man
plays again—and this difference in tone perhaps tells us
what is essential about this scene which is played with
Heidegger—he implies that when the *sprechen* of speech
is affected by a "ver-," it not only becomes a promisor,
but it also becomes unsettled, disturbed, corrupted, per-
verted, affected by a kind of fatal drift. You know that in
German the prefix "ver-" very often has this meaning.
And in fact the text on the *Social Contract* has just demonstrated (we will perhaps come to this soon) that aporetic structure which Paul de Man names an "allegory
of unreadability" in which the performative can be neither accomplished nor distinguished from a constative,
all the while remaining irreducible. The promise is impossible but inevitable. In a probably excessive formula
and which is not that of Paul de Man, we could almost
say this: even if a promise could be kept, this would
matter little. What is essential here is that a pure promise cannot properly take place, in a proper place, even
though promising is inevitable as soon as we open our
mouths—or rather as soon as there is a text, in a sense
precisely determined by this situation; and in fact, Paul
de Man insists upon the textual character of this "allegory of unreadability" by underlining this word: "the
pattern that identifies the *Social Contract* as a *textual*
allegory." This last phrase, moreover, says "This is why
textual allegories on this level of rhetorical complexity
generate history."

This last sentence seems important to me for
three reasons:

1. It assigns to textuality, as *versprechen* (the performative and generating perversion of the promise but
also, if we can say this, the *Ur-sprechen*), the condition of
the possibility and generation of history, and of historicity itself. No history without textual *versprechen*.

2. This last sentence can be read as an ironic signature, that is to say as a commitment and a promise which present themselves as a case of the law which this sentence states. Paul de Man knows that when we speak, we write *as* Rousseau, in the way he says the author of the *Social Contract* does, within this "misleading" of the *Versprechen* which nevertheless "conveys the promise of its own truth." Such a "signature" confirms: this is the last confirmation of the demonstration, and everything that we can say of it, what I say of it here, is already engaged, committed within the fatality of this "fact." As Rousseau, as Paul de Man, etc., and I will return to this "*as.*"

3. The *textual* allegory of unreadability comes almost at the conclusion of *Allegories of Reading.* As soon as allegory exists, these two expressions (allegory of reading, of the act of reading, of readingness (*lisance*), and allegory of unreadability *in the act*) are not contradictory. Their apparent contradiction is the *versprechen*, the promise at the origin of history.

We could play on the English word "lecture": this is an allegory of lecture rather than an allegory of reading. Some have asked why Paul de Man always speaks of reading rather than of writing. Well, perhaps because the allegory of reading is writing—or the inverse. But perhaps also because every reading finds itself caught, engaged precisely by the promise of saying the truth, by a promise which will have taken place with the very first word, within a scene of signature which is a scene of writing. It is not enough to say, as we have so often done, that every reading is writing, it is necessary to demonstrate it: following, for example, this structure of the promise. *Allegory of Reading*—this means many things in the book which bears this title: the scene of reading represented in the abyssal structure of a text, the allegory of "unreadability," "textual allegory," etc. You cannot read without speaking, speak without promising, promise without writing, write without reading that you have already promised even before you begin to speak, etc. And you can only take note of this, in other words, note as *acte*, before every act. You can only say and sign: yes, yes in memory of yes.

Paul de Man says that this allegory is "metafigural" since it is an allegory of a figure—for example, metaphor—"which relapses into the figure it deconstructs" (p. 275). The fact that this figural metafigurality, as the figure of deconstruction, is finally the very dimension of textuality at the same time that it is the upheaval of history is clearly what determines what happens to the *Sprechen* (let us say the Heideggerian *Sprechen*, that of *die Sprache spricht*) when it must, always already, give itself up to and be affected by the *versprechen*. This cannot not happen to it; from the origin on, it is destined to it; this is its destination, even though the *versprechen* threatens destination in it. And this threat comes to it as a text, as writing, through the event of signature, a signature which can only promise itself, and can only (inevitably) promise itself insofar as the path toward its destination is barred, within a no-exit, without end, a dead-end, the impasse of the aporia. These accidents are essential, they do not happen to the *sprechen* from the outside. Or rather, the outside does not accidentally come to the *sprechen* from the outside. Speaking affects itself from the outside ("La parole s'affecte du *dehors*"—I do not know if this sentence admits translation). This is why Paul de Man writes: *Die Sprache verspricht* (*sich*). He puts the reflexive pronoun within parentheses. He adds the pronoun as that which speech must add to itself in order to speak. This addition only appears in the essay's second version. I do not know if it is the correction of a typographical error. There was another in the same line. But this first version, which I read in the offprint that Paul de Man had given to me in September, 1976, said only *Die Sprache verspricht.* The last version, in *Allegories of Reading,* adds the word *sich*; but as soon as it does so the *self,* the relation that speech has with itself passes, if we can say this, through the *aporia* of a promise which never occurs, which never happens, but which cannot not occur; in other words, being unable to come forward or take place, the "sich" is itself at the same time constituted and de-constituted, deconstructed, if you wish, by the very *act* of the promise. In truth, it is the value of the *act*—and of the truth—which thus deconstructs *itself,* the "se," the "itself" of auto-deconstruction does not escape what I will call the aporetic event. It is significant that Paul de Man has added, from one version to the other, or on his proofs, this *sich* between parentheses. But even if he had not done this, nothing would be changed, since the *sich,* this last-minute signature, is itself affected by the *Versprechen.* A necessary and impossible promise, the *sich* lets itself be effaced by itself; it is promised to the effacement that it promises itself. From one version to the next, the title of the text also changed. I had at first read it under the title "Political Allegory in Rousseau"; I have rediscovered it under the title "Promises (*Social Contract*)." I now close this very long exergue.

Can we make a promise in a foreign language? He who says "I" in Blanchot's *L'Arrêt de Mort* feels himself to be irresponsible when he commits himself, making a promise in the language of the other.

A title is a promise, but it aggravates the *sich ver-*

sprechen. In giving the French title *Mémoires* to this series of lectures, I wanted to make a promise in my own
language, the promise would therefore be more serious;
but this language is not yours—of course many among
you speak French as if it were your native language—
and I speak to you at this moment within that dimension of the *übersetzen* wherein Gasché has remarkably
situated the stakes of Paul de Man's work. If I want,
then, to at least pretend to keep an impossible promise,
and to sign, it is necessary that I justify my title. The
deleted article and mark of the plural lend to this noun,
"Mémoires," within the contextual wilderness which
surrounds a title, its greatest potential for equivocation.
The perversion of language is at its peak here. You know
that in French the word *mémoire* has different meanings
according to whether one uses it in the masculine or the
feminine form. It is very rare that the same word can
have both a masculine and feminine form. In French,
mémoire is hybrid or androgynous (which is not true of
Mnemosyne or Mnēmē, nor of the nouns *Gedächtnis* or
memory). And the mark of the number (singular or plural) does not concern number but the very meaning of
the word. We say "une mémoire," la mémoire, in the
feminine, in order to designate, in its most general
sense, the faculty (psychological or not), the aptitude,
the place, the gathering of memories or thoughts, but it
is also the name of what we are seeking to think here
and which we have so much trouble grasping. In any
case, there are phrases which we can make only with
the feminine singular form. And these phrases are always concerned with "memories" which have no essential need for writing in its everyday sense. As to
the masculine form, it can have two meanings, each
different from the other and different from *la mémoire,*

according to whether it is in the singular or the plural form. *Un mémoire* (masculine singular) is a document, a report, a "memo," a memorandum, a balance sheet recording what must be remembered; it is always short and supposes some writing, an exposition from the outside, a spatial inscription. The acts of a colloquium or a convention are of this kind. The word "mémoires" (masculine plural), if it does not simply designate a *plurality* of *mémoires* in the form of documents, reports, balance sheets or acts (that is, "mémoire" in the preceding sense), and in those cases when this word is used *only* in the plural, again has to do with writings but this time it refers to those writings which tell of a life or a history of which the author can bear witness. This word is what you translate by "memoirs" (dropping the "e" and the accent), and most often these are related to that enigmatic genre of which we spoke the day before yesterday, to that genre which, according to Paul de Man, is not a genre: autobiography. For example, *Mémoires d'Outre-Tombe* or those "mémoires de ma vie" of which Rousseau speaks in a letter: "As to the memoirs of my life of which you speak to me, they are difficult to write without compromising anyone".[3] For reasons that we have noted, these *mémoires,* which are not necessarily confessional, are always and structurally *mémoires d'outre-tombe,* memoirs from beyond the grave.

This strange noun or name therefore has semantic species or varieties marked by number and genre. The "same" name can be used in a certain sense only in the feminine, in another sense only in the masculine, and its third sense can be stated only in the masculine plural.

By leaving this word in the plural and without an article in the title of these lectures, I was giving a sup-

plementary and still more equivocal use of the "s"
which would be able to cover or envelop the three uses
of this word and mark-over the possible plurality of
these uses, which would be able to cite them, as it were,
in advance. As if I were promising you that I would
concern myself with this very plurivocity and with cov-
ering the entire semantic or thematic field of *la mémoire.*
The translation of this title remains therefore impossible, each English word would have amputated a meaning or a body of possible phrases from this name. Those
who know me a little know that I was not announcing
my "memoirs" under this title; but this already supposes a contextual determination which, because it cannot be printed on the cover of a book, we cannot be sure
would not be open to misunderstanding. In fact would
this really be a misunderstanding? Is not what I here
dedicate to the memory of Paul de Man a mournful
fragment of my own memoirs and of my own memory?
I speak of the cover of a book because "memoirs," unlike *la mémoire,* also imply written exposition, in the
everyday sense of this term.

 This semantico-grammatical multiplicity is inscribed within the French idiom. Let us not hasten to
consider it as a pure dispersion. There is perhaps a principle of organization within this heterogeneity; it orders
itself around a diacritical rule, the discrimination between what can be said in the masculine and what can
be said only in the feminine. The two masculine values
(singular or plural) of *mémoire* always suppose a recourse to a spatial inscription, let us say to the written
mark, in the everyday sense of the term. Whereas the
feminine, *la mémoire,* even if it is pluralized, does not
necessarily imply this graphical or technical recourse.
We can traverse this discriminating line through a figure

(one could say "metaphorically") and speak of a writing of *la mémoire,* a writing of memory, as Montaigne does, for example, among many others, when he says: "Good memory is scriptural, it retains its figure." But here it is a rhetorical figure which poses all the problems that you can imagine, those of the transfer of the inside to the outside, of the soul to the body, and so on. And this figure is not the one of which Montaigne speaks, which here indicates written forms, marks engraved within memory *as* on paper.

If I have left the title, *Mémoires,* to its destiny as an untranslatable idiom, it is no doubt in order to say all of this, but also, and above all, in order to welcome what the signature of a promise keeps untranslatable by taking note of a proper name, that of Paul de Man. And I had to signal this tribute within the untranslatable idiom of my own language. Otherwise, I could have chosen another word, in English, also trembling in the body of its plurivocity. And it would be consonant with the "memorial" of this event (here I write the word "memorial" in two languages at the same time, the only difference being that of an accent, or of two accents, the one spoken, the other written). The English word, which I could have chosen for a title, would in my eyes have had only two inconveniences. Its French homonym has a very different meaning and, above all, I would have been unable to find it all alone, supposing that a word can be found and that one could ever find it all alone. The word, then, is *memento,* which in French primarily signifies an exterior mark destined to recall a memory (*souvenir*). My title was already announced and the first two lectures were written when a letter from David Carroll informed me that the breadth of this word would have been able to comprehend, under its folds, in

English, all that I meant to say and do here. I cite David
Carroll citing the Oxford English Dictionary:

Memento pl. mementoes
1. Eccl. Either of the two prayers in the Canon of the mass in
which the living and the departed are respectively commem-
orated [I verified, at least according to the *Littré*, that this
usage is also possible in French: "A Catholic liturgical term.
The memento of the living, the memento of the dead, two
prayers of the Canon of the mass, the one for the living, the
other for the dead. E. Lat. *memento,* remember, souviens-toi:
as an order, an imperative. *Memini* is a perfect form coming
from the radical *man,* sanscrit *manmi,* I think, I know,
whence *memini,* I have known, I remember myself (see
mental)." The *Littré* thus inscribes, in the name of the radical,
the name of *man,* the name de Man].
2. A reminder, warning, or hint as to conduct or with regard
to *future events* [my emphasis, JD]. Obs.
        b. concr. An object serving to remind or warn in this
way.
3. Something to remind one of a past event or condition of
an absent person, of something that once existed, now chiefly
an object kept as a memorial of some person or event.
        b. A memory or remembrance. Obs. rare
4. Humorously misused for: a) a reverie, a doze b) (one's)
memory.

If a dividing line orders this multiplicity of usages, and if
it passes through the supposed opposition between the
interiority of memory and the (graphic, spatial, technical) exteriority of memory or of memories as archives,
documents, acts, etc., we have just rediscovered—let us
say, recalled—the redoubtable problem of *Gedächtnis*
and *Erinnerung*. Where does the provocative force of de
Manian interpretation reside? In at least this: that in
order to distinguish *Gedächtnis* (thinking memory) from

Erinnerung (interiorizing memory), whether he does it in the name of Hegel or by focusing on some "cornerstone" of the Hegelian system, de Man marks the irreducible link between thought as memory and the technical dimension of memorization, the art of writing, of "material" inscription, in short, of all that exteriority which, after Plato, we call hypomnesic, the exteriority of Mnemon, rather than that of Mnēmē. In recalling this unity between thought and technology (that is to say, as well, between thought *and* the exteriority of the graphic inscription—de Man speaks of the "art of writing"—between thought and techno-science) through memory, de Manian deconstruction resembles, in the same act, a double decision. Very schematically: *on the one hand,* it in principle gives itself the means to not drive out into the exterior and inferior dark regions of thought, the immense question of artificial memory and of the modern modalities of archivation which today affects, according to a rhythm and with dimensions that have no common measure with those of the past, the totality of our relation to the world (on this side of or beyond its anthropological determination): habitat, all languages, writing, "culture," art (beyond picture galleries, film libraries, video libraries, record libraries), literature (beyond libraries), all information or informatization (beyond "memory" banks of givens), techno-sciences, philosophy (beyond university institutions) and everything within the transformation which affects all relations to the future. This prodigious mutation not only heightens the stature, the quantitative economy of so-called artificial memory, but also its qualitative structure—and in doing so it obliges us to rethink what relates this artificial memory to man's so-called psychical and interior memory, to truth, to the simulacrum and simulation of truth, etc. Let it be quickly said in passing that, if we wish to analyze that nebula named "deconstruction in America," it is necessary *also,* not only, but also, to take account of this problematic under all of its aspects. There is no deconstruction which does not begin by tackling this problematic or by preparing itself to tackle this problematic, and which does not begin by again calling into question the dissociation between thought and technology, especially when it has a hierarchical vocation, however secret, subtle, sublime or denied it may be. This leads me to the second point: *on the other hand,* in fact, the attention accorded to this link between *Gedächtnis* and hypomnesic writing no doubt leads to our no longer being able to subscribe (for my part, I have never done so) to Heidegger's sentence and to all that it supposes: *Die Wissenschaft denkt nicht,* science does not think. This is a phrase written and often reconsidered, meditated upon, and prudently explicated by Heidegger in the parts of the text of *Was heisst Denken* on *Gedächtnis* and *Gedanc,* which I quoted a little while ago. I would not want my treatment of this phrase to be a preterition and thus neglect its force or its necessity, but I cannot here retrace the path which has led to it or which supports it. Let us say very quickly, perhaps too quickly, that despite the precautions he takes, and that have the form of denial, Heidegger marks within this phrase the rigorous necessity of an essential exteriority and of an implicit hierarchy between, on the one hand, thought as memory (*Denken, Gedächtnis, Gedanc*) and, on the other hand, science, but also technology, writing and even literature. We would be able to find numerous indications of this in *Was heisst Denken* itself. No doubt Heidegger defends himself by thus instituting a simple division ("on the one hand, on the other hand") and

ACTS

109

by accompanying this with an anti-scientific, anti-technical evaluation which would lead us to subordinate or play down everything which is not "the thinking of the thinker": "Science does not think in the sense in which a thinker thinks. Still, it does not at all follow that thinking has no need of turning towards the sciences. The statement 'science does not think' does not imply a license under which thinking is free to set itself up, so to speak, offhandedly, by simply thinking something up" (Eng. 134; Ger. 154). This prevents neither Heidegger's division from persisting in all its rigor, nor hierarchy. What refers to science here also goes for technology ("Modern science grounds itself upon the essence of technology"). The Heideggerian argument which operates everywhere to justify this division and hierarchy, when it is reduced to its essential schema, has the following form and can be transposed everywhere: "The essence of technology is nothing technological." The thinking of this essence therefore is in no way "technological" or "technicist"; it is free of all technicity because it thinks technicity, it is not scientific because it thinks the scientificity of science. Heidegger would say the same thing of all determined sciences, for example, of linguistics, rhetoric, etc. The thinking of the rhetoricity of rhetoric (within the history of philosophy, a derived and belated technological knowledge) is in no way a rhetoric.

Perhaps we can measure the stakes of de Manian interpretation. It delineates a gesture quite different from that of Heidegger by recalling that the relation of *Gedächtnis* to technique, artifice, writing, the sign, etc., could not be one of exteriority or heterogeneity. This amounts to saying that the exteriority or the division, the dis-junction, *is the relation*, the essential juncture between thinking memory and the so-called techno-scientific, indeed literary outside (for literature, literary writing, is, for Heidegger, in the same position as techno-science with regard to thought or poetry).[4] I would say that this gesture is quite different from Heidegger's and that it gives rise to quite different intonations. This is undoubtedly so, but things are never so simple and we ought to give ourselves the time and have the patience outside of a "lecture" to follow all the folds of these thoughts. I must limit myself here to two indications. On the side of deconstruction, if this can be said, and in its de Manian form, a certain continuity (*within* the disjunctive structure) between thinking memory and techno-scientific memory does not exclude, but, on the contrary, permits a thinking of the essence of tech-nology, a thinking which it is not within the logic of deconstruction to renounce. This is why this deconstruc-tion, at the very moment when it puts in question the hierarchical division between thought and technology, is neither technicist nor technological. But on the other side, that of Heidegger, things are not any simpler. It is in fact difficult to reconcile precisely this hierarchical division with the principle of other propositions every bit as essential to Heidegger. For example: the affirma-tion according to which there is no "meta-language" (*Unterwegs zur Sprache*) should, in principle, undermine the possibility of this hierarchical division. It would be the same for that thinking of the *Gedanc*, for it also escapes a delimitation opposing the outside to the in-side from the point of view of representation, that is to say, from a point of view determining thought as inte-rior representation or as interiorizing memory (*Erin-nerung*): "The *Gedanc* means soul, heart, the bottom of the heart (*Herzensgrund*), the innermost essence of man which reaches outward most fully and towards the outermost limits, and so decisively that, rightly thought, the representation of an interior and an exterior does not arise" (Eng. 144; Ger. 157).

But all this does not proceed in Heidegger—and we have just recalled this—without decisive recourse to an originality of thinking, to the purity of the "pure thinker" (Socrates), of a *Sprache* which speaks (*spricht*) before promising itself or before going astray in an impossible promise (*sich versprechen*), without recourse, finally, to the originary meaning of names or words. Now what is it that distinguishes, in this respect, the style of de Manian deconstruction, as is indicated in an increasingly more accentuated way in the texts of *Allegories of Reading?* Well, among other things, an unprecendented bringing into play and at the same time a subversive reelaboration of Austinian theorems and of speech act theory, which in de Man's work at the same time progresses and enters a crisis. We could show—at another time—why this movement was indispensable for a rigorous deconstruction. If, for the moment, we only wish to signal the change of style or tone with regard to the Heideggerian meditation on *Gedächtnis* or *Gedanc* (we will go further in a minute), we can rely on this indication: here the interest is in texts, in textual figures (*textual allegories,* for example) and not in the originality of a *Sprache* before any *Versprechen;* here the interest is in textualization or contextualization rather than the original meaning of the name. Let us take an example and let us cite Austin, since he represents here another pole and another style.

Since the day before yesterday, we appear, at the very least, to have been asking: what does memory mean? And from time to time we seem to have been reducing this question to the following one: what does the word "mémoire" signify? In the same way we could have asked: what does the word "deconstruction" signify? It has even occurred to us to consult the dictionary, but in passing and without having too much confidence in it. Neither Heidegger nor Austin believe that the meanings of words are found in dictionaries, not even in etymological dictionaries. But for apparently different, even opposed reasons. Heidegger thinks that it is necessary *to think* the meaning of words in order to be able to read and examine a dictionary. Austin says, in no uncertain terms, that words do *not* have a meaning, and that it is absurd to look in a dictionary for something like the *given* meaning of a word. Only sentences have a meaning, and the dictionary can only help by informing us about the sentences wherein conventions authorize the usage of these words. This is practically what Wittgenstein says in the first words of the *Blue Book*. It would be very necessary, but I must renounce doing it here, to slowly and minutely question Austin's *"The Meaning of a Word"*,[5] a text to which, it seems to me, de Man never refers. This essay was also a lecture. It was even given twice and I wonder how the essay's essential and constant recourse to quotation marks, italics and parentheses was transposed (or written on the blackboard).

This lecture had also a title which is not a sentence, *The meaning of a word*. It does not begin with sentences, but with two tables, two lists of "specimens of sense" and "specimens of nonsense." At the head of the second list is the sentence "What-is-the-meaning-of-a-word?" After having written this double list, Austin declares that many readers probably already see all or part of what he will say. But he is going to say it anyway because not *every*one sees the *totality* of what he will say, some of them get it slightly wrong; and also, there is a "tendency to forget it." So much so that the author of the "paper" justifies his purpose and the *act* of his lecture through this empiricism and essential differentialism (not everyone understands everything to the same degree in the same way, there is no simple alternative between understanding and not understanding, only the complex relations between the whole and the part, etc.). But he also justifies the act of his lecture *"The Meaning of a Word"* by the "tendency to forget," and to forget what we know, what we see, what we understand, indeed, even what we love or approve of, to forget the "meaning" of all of this as well as to forget the sentences that we produce on this subject. The act of this lecture will thus also be an act of memory, a *memento*: remember, don't only agree with me; remember that you have understood what I have told you, that you have approved it; promise me and promise yourself to remember it. Now, what is it here that we have an irrepressible tendency to forget each time we open our mouths, to forget then even when we know it? The fact that a word does not have a "meaning." Only a "sentence" can have "meaning." Before making this "preliminary remark," Austin will have introduced this extraordinary scene of rhetoric, as naïve as it is cunning, cunningly playing with naïveté, through a battery of performative acts, primary or not, which would deserve a long study: promises and excuses. After having promised and *made* us promise (for example, not to forget), he excuses himself to those who are already converted. But at the same time he does not excuse himself, since the converts too have need of a *memento*:

I begin, then, with some remarks about "the meaning of a word." I think many persons now see [after reading the lists

of specimens, I suppose, on the blackboard] all or part of
what I shall say: but not all do, and there is a tendency to
forget, or to get it slightly wrong. In so far as I am merely
flogging the converted, I apologize to them. (*PP,* p. 56)

Me too. This is perhaps the principal reason why
I cite Austin here. Because of the promise, the memento,
and the excuse—on the subject of a word, *Mémoires,*
which perhaps has no "meaning." But can we promise
or excuse ourselves by citing the promise or excuse of
another? Can we do this without citation?

Between the list of specimens and these excuses,
followed by the "preliminary remark" according to
which "properly speaking, what alone has a meaning is
a *sentence,*" we find a short paragraph which could well
be the most interesting part of the "paper": nine lines
which claim to summarize and describe what is going to
follow:

This paper is about the phrase "the meaning of a word." It is
divided into three parts, of which the first is the most trite
and the second the most muddled: all are too long [you see
that he is in the process of describing my lectures and of
excusing me for them, J.D.]. In the first, I try to make it clear
that the phrase "the meaning of a word" is, *in general* [I
emphasize *in general* as I had emphasized *properly speaking* a
little while ago], *if not always,* a dangerous nonsense phrase.
In the other two parts I consider in turn two questions, often
asked in philosophy, which clearly need new and careful
scrutiny if that facile phrase "the meaning of a word" is no
longer to be permitted to impose upon us.(ibid.)

We can read this text as a text of law, the ethico-
political project of a text of law interdicting or de-
legitimizing, at least among philosophers, the future recourse to a phrase, let us say a locution, which is some-

times "dangerous," which is *generally* dangerous and which should, if we are convinced by Austin and if we do not forget his demonstration, "no longer . . . be permitted to impose upon us." What he proposes to delegitimize here is the very thing he promises to speak to us about and which gives title to his lecture, not only the title to be pronounced (and twice rather than once), which would justify this act and its repetition "for memory," but also, in the strict sense, his title, "the meaning of a word."

A title is always a promise. Here the title does not constitute a "sentence." It therefore has no "meaning." It acts out a "promise" in a statement which "properly speaking" has no "meaning." This title is therefore dangerous, especially for the community of philosophers; it has only an improper and figural "meaning." Is this title not a literary parasite which, promising nothing philosophical, in the last instance, announces that we will hear for an hour or two a certain number of "sentences" in which, by playing with old and new philosophemes, the phrase, the locution "the meaning of a word" will be pronounced with a great number of variations, with or without quotation marks, italics or hyphens, with or without *meaning?* But this literary fiction, if it really is one, nonetheless would seek (and up to a certain point, successfully) to produce political effects and change conventions, to legitimize or de-legitimize, to constitute, through its very irony, a new right. In any case, this fiction cannot be *totally* grounded in existing conventions in order to define sentences in which a word has "meaning." This is because everything depends upon contexts which are always open, non-saturable, because a single word (for example, a word in a title) begins to bear the meaning of all the potential phrases

in which it is to be inscribed (and therefore begins to
promise, to violently ground its own right and other
conventions, since it does not yet *totally* have the right to
promise) and because, inversely, no phrase has an abso-
lutely determinable "meaning": it is always in the situation of the word or title in relation to the text which
borders it and which carries it away, in relation to the
always open context which always promises it more
meaning. What I am saying here goes for the words
"mémoire" or "deconstruction" but also for so-called
proper names.

One of the things I like in Austin's text is that at
bottom he does not leave any properly philosophical
thesis in place—and therefore any properly philosophical institution. This is the part of his legacy the least
understood by his official, that is to say his presumptive,
heirs. He speaks and finally confesses to speaking improperly, figurally, of the conditions in which a word
could have a "meaning." But he speaks of and confesses
these conditions improperly, he promises improperly,
and he improperly remembers, has us promise to remember, in the least certain circumstances, and with as
little assurance as possible. His sentences resemble
those words which never have enough meaning or—
like a title—they have too much. He is finally content
with saying: there are dangers, there are "uncanny"
(*unheimlich*) things, there are curious beliefs and odd
views, *there is this:* for example "there is the curious
belief that all words are names, i.e. in effect *proper*
names [this is a gesture essential to deconstruction, it
was perhaps its primary gesture: to wonder at that
"curious belief"!], and therefore stand for something or
designate it in the way that a proper name does. But this
view that general names 'have denotation' in the same

way that proper names do, is quite as odd as the view
that proper names 'have connotation' in the same way
that general names do, which is commonly recognized
to lead to error" (p. 61). Whereupon he speaks of a
"more common malady . . ."

I do not have the time to devote to *"The Meaning
of a Word,"* neither the time nor analytic patience that it
deserves. Before leaving it, provisionally, and by promising to return to it, I will again recall *two things,* two
partial and particular things, within the exemplary figure of metonymy:

I. I will at first underline two *odd* examples with
which Austin illustrates his purpose. Both, in a certain
way, evoke, *on the one hand,* death and suicide, and, *on
the other hand,* writing and the necessity of a new idiom.
I quote here several lines without having the time to
analyze them:

A. Now suppose I ask my third question "What is the
point of doing *anything*—not anything *in particular,* but just
anything?" Old Father William would no doubt kick me
downstairs without the option [he has just patiently answered these odd, but "decidable," questions, leaving room
for an "option"]. But lesser men, raising this same question
and finding no answer, would very likely commit suicide or
join the Church. (luckily, in the case of "What is the meaning
of a word" the effects are less serious, amounting only to the
writing of books). On the other hand, more adventurous in-
tellects would no doubt take to asking "What is the-point-of-
doing-a-thing?" or "What is the "point" of doing a thing." (p.
59) [I let you imagine Heidegger's questions, at least their
style, in terms of what this supposes of a thinking of *doing*
(*l'acte*) and of the *thing*].

B. Supposing now someone says "x is extended but
has no shape." Somehow we cannot see what this "could
mean"—there is no semantic convention, explicit or implicit,

118   ACTS

to cover this case: yet it is not prohibited in any way—there
are no limiting rules about what we might or might not say *in
extraordinary cases* . . . we can only describe what it is we are
trying to imagine, by means of words which precisely describe and evoke the *ordinary* case, which we are trying to
think away. Ordinary language *blinkers* the already feeble
imagination. It would be difficult, in this way, if I were to say
"Can I think of a case where a man would be neither at home
nor not at home?" and get the answer, "No" when certainly
he is not at home. But supposing I happen *first* to think of the
situation when I call on him just after he has died: then I see
at once it would be wrong to say either. So in our case, the
only thing to do is to imagine or experience all kinds of odd
situations, and then suddenly turn round on oneself and ask:
there, *now* would I say that, being extended it must be
shaped? A new idiom might in odd cases be demanded.
[Imagine questions of another style, for example, of a
Heidegger: what is an odd case? what is an idiom, *eine
Sprache?* Who will speak it and how, if not *die Sprache selbst?*
But what happens if "Die Sprache verspricht (sich)"? What
do you mean by all these words and names? Is death an "odd
case" and am I not still in the process of evoking someone
"after he has died" and of recalling him again. Is this an
"ordinary case" or an "extraordinary case"? I close the pa-
renthesis]. A little further on, Austin says: "Very often philosophers are only engaged on this task, when they seem to
be perversely using words in a way which makes no sense
according to 'ordinary usage.' There may be extraordinary
facts, even about our everyday experience, which plain men
and plain language overlook." (pp. 68-69)

2. Second reminder. "The meaning of a word"
demonstrates for us—and this demonstration is also a
reminder—the irreducibility of the structure of promise
in every language, even in the language that would
want to speak the truth of the promise or of those par-

ticular kinds of *speech acts* which are explicit promises. We have also just seen why this *arche-promise,* which promises truth and meaning, is finally neither true nor meaningful in its proper and originary moment: it is the moment of the name or of the word alone, of the title which promises and pledges out of its insignificance or its limited meaning. This is the moment of the given word, this before all else. This moment calls for new conventions which it itself proposes or promises, but which, for that reason, it cannot without artifice take advantage of or found its authority on at the very moment it calls, when it calls for new laws. And every theorem on *speech acts,* for example, any theorem on the distinction between performative and constative, and in particular on the promise, already proceeds as a promise, a promise of truth, with all the paradoxes and aporias which can attend such an approach. This ethico-juridical or historico-political dimension is not absent from *The Meaning of a Word,* since there it is a question of "dangerous" phrases, of "permission" to be given or refused, and conventions to be created. We are in fact at that place where the possibility is announced for political, ethical, juridical, historical language.

If I have chosen to touch briefly upon this text by Austin, it is for numerous reasons. I will note two of them. It is impossible to imagine a problematic or rhetoric more removed from those of Heidegger than Austin's. Now, Paul de Man's idiom, his "deconstructionist" style is neither Heideggerian nor Austinian even if it mobilizes and, above all, displaces, crosses, and decenters both traditions at the same time. Some might want to minimize the novelty of this scene by saying that he has translated the two traditions the one into the other; and as they both have their heritage and their institu-

tions in America, Paul de Man's work here is at once
bold and useful. But such a translation is much more
than a translation, it upsets (*dérange*) each of the two
axiomatics which it appears to translate or transfer, it
mobilizes others, it does not belong to either, and it
writes a new text which therefore at first appears unreadable or unacceptable to both sides, at least in what
in it is most new. It upsets everyone (*Il dérange tout le
monde*).
    I am perhaps wrong in speaking of axiomatics in
relation to Heidegger and Austin. They both comment
upon the subject of those promises which are axiomatics. Let us say that these commentaries are themselves
promises; Paul de Man's makes another kind of promise
on the subject of promise.
    The other reason is that we perhaps get a better,
more economical introduction to the idiom of de Manian deconstruction by asking what it has *done,* through
its actions, to the Austinian theory of *speech acts.*
Rodolphe Gasché has said something essential and incontestable about this. From another point of view, so
has Suzanne Gearhart. I do not know if what I will
suggest about it will be different but, in any case, it will
not be, I believe, in contradiction with what they have
already said.
    If we were authorized to speak of a second period
of de Manian thought, we might notice there, at first
glance, a sort of acceptance and appropriation of the
motif and word "deconstruction": the word appears
more and more frequently in his work and it would be
necessary to record and to analyze all its values, for I
believe them to be multiple. And simultaneously, a first
glance would detect the new insistence of an important
debate (*Auseinandersetzung*) with the Austinian opposi-

tion between the performative and the constative; an opposition confirmed, developed, implanted, well beyond its original field—and then immediately undermined and made sterile in its very principle. This dispute is primarily a deconstruction, not only of the Austinian text, but of the axiomatics and theorems of the theory of *speech acts:* which does not mean that we can or that we should renounce them. But we must take note of the aporetic and allegorical structure of the act in a *speech act.*

I just said: "If we were authorized to speak of a second period . . . ." This is a classic and inevitable question which will not, in this case any more than in others, receive a satisfying answer. On this question, again, Rodolphe Gasché and Suzanne Gearhart are no doubt right when they speak, the one of discontinuity, the other of continuity. Paul de Man has often criticized, or at least considered as fictions, all "periodizations." He says this already in "The Rhetoric of Blindness" (*Blindness and Insight, p. 137*). This commentary on "periods," whether it is a question of an individual work or of Western metaphysics, always has the value of a fiction or of a story we tell ourselves in order to dramatize, historically and teleologically, a non-historical argument. Must we in the same way prohibit ourselves from "periodizing" Paul de Man's itinerary? He does not himself say that we have no right to do this, but it is necessary to know that we are in this way undertaking a figurative and narrative interpretation.

I will not risk dwelling on this question for too long, only the time necessary to pose a suspended question on the subject of the motif of "deconstruction" in the interrupted work of Paul de Man. Even if it cannot resolve his work, this question is indissociable from that of "deconstruction in America": from every possible point of view (I will try to enumerate these later), "deconstruction in America" would not be what it is without Paul de Man. Now what happens in the very inside of his work, if we can isolate this, between (1) the moments when he does not speak of deconstruction, (2) those when he speaks of it as an operation taking place in *other* texts, and (3) those when he presents his own work as a deconstruction? You know that he does this in *Allegories of Reading* and that he comments on his own periodized path: he does this a first time in his "Preface" to *Allegories of Reading* and another time in his "Foreword to the Revised, Second Edition of *Blindness and Insight.*" I refer you to these two texts which include an invaluable periodizing auto-interpretation, to be read also as memoirs or as a theoretical autobiography, with the fictive, ironic, or allegorical dimension that de Man's signature imprints on all his texts.

By letting you reread these "mémoires" in the form of a preface, I will be content to point out a few dividing lines. In the second "Foreword" to *Blindness and Insight,* Paul de Man declares his amnesia when he writes: "I am not given to retrospective self-examination and mercifully forget what I have written with the same alacrity I forget bad movies—although, as with bad movies, certain scenes or phrases return at times to embarrass and haunt me like a guilty conscience."[6] Again, the return of the ghost as text, or the text as ghost, you will recall what we said of this two days ago. Another dividing line is that which the first "Foreword" to *Blindness and Insight* recalls. The author presents himself as someone "whose teaching has been more or less evenly divided between the United States and Europe" (vii). And finally the last division whose line traverses the very history of *Allegories of Reading* is one its author

himself periodizes; and it is here precisely a question of
the "term 'deconstruction,' which has rapidly become a
label as well as a target. Most of this book was written
before 'deconstruction' became a bone of contention,
and the term is used here in a technical rather than a
polemical sense—which does not imply that it therefore
becomes neutral or ideologically innocent. But I saw no
reason to delete it."

Why this scene of deletion of the "I saw no reason to delete it," this "I will not erase" (further on there
is an "I do not wish to erase" and the book's dedication
also speaks to me of the "unerasable"), why this risk of
erasure and this affirmation in the form of a signature,
of a promise or commitment ("I will not erase")—do
they have, well beyond biographies, through autobiographies, an essential relation with the text of deconstruction? I will not return to this problem in terms
of generalities. Let us situate it within Paul de Man's
singular trajectory. We cannot write what we do not
wish to erase, we can only promise it in terms of what
can always be erased. Otherwise, there would be neither memory nor promise.

Now the word "deconstruction" could have been
erased in thousands of different ways. I will not speak of
my complicated relations with the inscription and erasure of this word. But look at Paul de Man: he begins by
saying that finally "there is no need to deconstruct
Rousseau"[7] for the latter has already done so himself.
This was another way of saying: there is always already
deconstruction, at work *in* works, especially in *literary*
works. Deconstruction cannot be applied, after the fact
and from the outside, as a technical instrument of modernity. Texts deconstruct *themselves* by themselves, it is
enough to recall it or to recall them to oneself.

I felt myself, up to a certain point, rather in

agreement with this interpretation that I extend even beyond so-called literary texts—on the condition that we agree on the "itself" of "deconstructs itself" and on this self of "the recalling to oneself". It is perhaps the reading of this little used word "itself" ("se") which supports the entire reading of Rousseau, and displaces it from the first to the last texts, from *Blindness and Insight* to *Allegories of Reading*. I myself have often elaborated on this point; the interest of the question is not there. But what is happening then in Paul de Man's work when the word "deconstruction," which could have or should have been erased by itself, since it only designates the explicitation of a relation of the work to *itself*, instead of erasing itself inscribes itself more and more, whether it is a question of the number of times it occurs, of the variety or of the prominence of the sentences which give it meaning? I do not have an answer to this question. Always already, as Paul de Man says, there is deconstruction at work in the work of Rousseau, even if Rousseau abstained from saying a word about it, from saying the word. Always already, there is deconstruction at work in the work of Paul de Man, even during the period when he did not speak of it or during the time when he spoke of it in order to say that there was nothing new to say about it.

But what of this "always already" when we judge it both possible and necessary to say of what is said, that it goes without saying? Always already, it was said, there was deconstruction at work in history, culture, literature, philosophy, in short, in Western memory in its two continents. And I believe that this is true; we could show it in each discourse, each work, each system, each moment. But what of this "always already" when deconstruction receives this name, proper as it may be and when—somewhere, at a given moment—it becomes not only a theme but also a "topos" of which we do not know whether or not it must produce a system, particular methods, a certain kind of teaching, institutions, etc., and which, in any case, produces conflicts? when these latter are not only theoretical, but also passionate, symbolic, political, etc? It is necessary to recognize that this happens (*es ereignet sich . . .*). In the case of Paul de Man, as much as in that of "deconstruction in America," the "always already" which tends to erase the singularity of the event is erased in its turn before the signature of this word. As precarious as this signature is, it asserts itself as history insofar as the origin of its"taking-place" is unlocatable. I do not have a formalizable answer to this question. But it is posed to us by the history of deconstruction and by history as deconstruction.

Rousseau: this is not one proper name among others in de Manian deconstruction. This is why I recall it now. The first moment of the *Auseinandersetzung* with the word and motif of deconstruction traverses, as you know, Paul de Man's reading of Rousseau. This is the important essay entitled "The Rhetoric of Blindness," which proposes an original and new reading of Rousseau, defines that concept of the "rhetoric of blindness" which organizes all of the work in the book, and disputes a reading of Rousseau that I had proposed in a recently published book. I will not enter here into this debate, for many reasons. First of all, because it still remains a bit enigmatic to me. Next, because others, including Paul de Man, have themselves returned to this debate and have done so better than I could do it here. I again think of Rodolphe Gasché, Suzanne Gearhart, Richard Klein, David Carroll. Finally, and above all, if there must be a last word on this debate, I want it to come today from Paul de Man. I can only, from now on, speak of him in the desire to speak to him, in the desire to speak with him and, finally, to leave to him the chance to speak. Our memories intersect here; I will not touch directly on this public debate, but speak indirectly of it for a very brief moment in order to make a few private remarks.

First remark. In Europe and in America, whether or not it is a question of deconstruction, I have had the luck or the bad luck, as Paul de Man did, and often conjointly with him, to provoke violent and numerous reactions: as we say, "Critiques." Now, never has any appeared to me as generous in its rigor, as free of all reactiveness, as respectful of the future without ever giving way to complaisance, never has any criticism appeared to me so easy to accept as that of Paul de Man in "The Rhetoric of Blindness." None has ever given me so much to think about as his has, even if I did not feel I was in agreement with it; though I was not simply in disagreement with it either. I no longer remember, and it matters little, what I wrote in answer to Paul de Man, in order to thank him and probably to argue a bit, in a letter of which the only thing that I today remember is that I wrote it to him from Oxford. But in order to let Paul de Man have the say, I will permit myself to quote, if this is not too indiscreet—once will not make it a habit—a fragment from the letter that I received in answer to mine. This will, in this way, be much more interesting than what I was able to or would be able to say. Believe me, I have hesitated a great deal before doing this, and I hesitate again now: is it not abusive, violent, or indiscreet to quote from such letters, in however fragmentary a fashion? Is it sufficient to omit here, for the moment, everything that comes from personal memory, whether his or mine, and to limit oneself strictly, if this is possible, to what concerns a public exchange, here a certain reading of Rousseau? What made me decide to decide, to take the risk of deciding, is something that happened on February 25 of this year at the moment when I was at this very point in the preparation of these lectures. I will tell you its little story. While stirring up so many, many memories, I said to myself that day that Rousseau has played a singular role for Paul de Man and for me. And from the very first day of our meeting, in Baltimore in 1966, when we had begun with this: by evoking *l'Essai sur l'Origine des langues,* a text then little read and on which we were both in the process of working. Beginning with this memory, of which the only thing that I retain is the name Rousseau, I passed to the following remark: the entire—interrupted—history of de Manian deconstruction passes through Rousseau. We could follow this history from the first essay on "The Rhetoric of Blindness" up to the six texts of the last part of *Allegories of Reading* where a deconstructive staging (*mise en oeuvre*) of *speech acts* is unfolded. But no, I said then, if this is true, and I believe that it is true, it is also necessary to name Nietzsche, whose figure and thinking have assisted and insisted and haunted Paul de Man in a way just as unerasable as that of Rousseau. It is Rousseau *with* Nietzsche, and the latter provides a very certain reference for the analysis of the auto-biographico-political promise in the *Social Contract:* "All laws are future-oriented and prospective; their illocutionary mode is that of the promise.[21]"[Note 21: "In *The Genealogy of Morals,* Nietzsche also derives the notion of a transcendental referent (and the specificity of 'man') from the possibility of making promises" (*AR*, p. 273.] Rousseau-and-Nietzsche, then, and I said to myself that, curiously, this couple had always haunted me, me too, and well before I was in a position to refer to them in published works. Barely adolescent (here it comes, we are approaching the genre of "memoirs," in its worst form), I read them together and I confided my despair to a kind of diary: how was it possible for me to reconcile these two admirations and these two identifications since the one spoke so ill of the other? End of "memoirs" for today. Returning to Paul de Man, I said to myself then: yes, for him it had also been Rousseau and Nietzsche, all in all, the two bodies or two parts of *Allegories of Reading*. This is too obvious. I was then struck by another piece of evidence: there is a third figure in this, there is a third identification: Hölderlin. This time his and not mine. For reasons which here are of little consequence, my familiarity with Hölderlin remains a bit abstract, or it passes precisely through the family of Heidegger or the family of Paul de Man. Wait a minute, I said to myself then: Hölderlin between Rousseau and Nietzsche. What a trinity! But these are the three madmen of Western modernity! The three measurers of the immeasurable in terms of which Western modernity is measured. In this way, Paul de Man would have meditated all his life on the law and on the destiny of the West (the logos, rhetoric, promise, philosophy, literature, politics) in the company of these three madmen of the West (these "extraordinary cases," as Austin would perhaps have said), and by listening to their madness from a kind of American exile where one of his friends even nicknamed him "Hölderlin in America," etc. I daydreamed a bit on this theme of madness—the figure of de Manian thinking as a thinking of madness, a thinking memory or a history of a Western and modern madness, of a madness of America, not in the sense that America would be mad but in the sense that it is necessary to think it from the perspective of mad lucidity, under the light of lunacy. I daydreamed in these realms without knowing where I was going, and without knowing if I ought to go ahead and publish such fragments from a letter; at least this would interest friends, readers, or students of Paul de Man and add a public contribution to the debate surrounding Rousseau. I told myself then that it was necessary for me at least to reread all of these letters before deciding. And it is because I reread this letter, which touches precisely upon madness, that I believed, rightly or wrongly, I could ignore the prohibition against quoting from private correspondence. I repeat, I only draw from it what, finally, does not concern me. Here is a first fragment. It is from a letter dated July 9, 1970, from Zumikon in Switerland, before the publication of "The Rhetoric of Blindness." I had received the manuscript and I had written to thank Paul de Man, who answered me thus:

The other day was neither the time nor the place to speak again of Rousseau and I do not know if you have any reason to return to the question. Your supposed "agreement" [This is a word I must have written in my letter] can only be kindness, for if you object to what I say about metaphor, you must, as it should be, object to everything. My essay moves through, for economic reasons, a whole series of questions and complications which, in my eyes, do not weaken the central proposition. I do not yet know why you keep refusing Rousseau the value of radicality which you attribute to Mallarmé and no doubt to Nietzsche; I believe that it is for hermeneutic rather than historical reasons, but I am probably wrong. The text will appear in October in *Poétique* in a translation which seems to me faithful.

The text having appeared in *Poétique,* I must have thanked Paul de Man anew, since a letter from Zurich, some months later, dated January 4, 1971, said the following, in its turn a form of acknowledgement (this is still an extract; I could not erase, within the very inside of certain phrases and under the pretext that they were addressed to me, all the gestures of generous courtesy):

Your commentaries are to me all the more invaluable since I am still in the process of working on Rousseau (and Nietzsche). There is no disagreement between us about the basis of your thinking but a certain divergence in our way of nuancing and situating Rousseau. This divergence is important to me for the notions that I had come to about the question of writing before having had the benefit of your thinking, above all, they were drawn from Rousseau (and Hölderlin) [Second parenthesis: "Rousseau (and Nietzsche)" four lines above, "Rousseau (and Hölderlin)" here]. The desire to exempt Rousseau (as you say) *at all costs* from blindness is therefore, for me, a gesture of fidelity to my own itinerary. Rousseau has led me to a certain understanding which, due allowance being made, seems to me near to that which you have had the force to begin. And as *l'Essai sur l'origine des langues* is one of the texts upon which I have been relying for such a long time, I must have put a certain ardor into my defense of the relative insight which I have benefited from. This having been said, I did not wish to exempt Rousseau from blindness but only wished to show that, on the specific question of the rhetoricity of his writing, he was not blinded. This is what gives to his text the particular status that we would both agree, I believe, to call "literary." That this insight is accompanied by a perhaps more redoubtable blindness—and which could be, for example, madness—I didn't feel myself obliged to say about this latter text, but I would say it in regard to the *Dialogues* and especially in regard to *Emile,* which seems to me one of the most demented texts there is.[8]

The rest of the letter concerns "specific points":

> It is sometimes a simple question of formulation. I have not, for example, wanted to say that "sound" would be the referent of music but, paraphrasing Rousseau, that silence, as the negation of sound, can be. As to the principal question, that of signification as a void, as the failure or refusal of meaning, I do not believe that we are in disagreement on this. I admit that, within the polemical convention adopted in the essay, I have dialecticized too little, but this is because your version of Rousseau operates, in fact, from the opposite extreme. I incessantly return to this in what I am in the process of trying to do with Rousseau and Nietzsche and perhaps we can speak of this again later.

This was written in 1971 and I believe that we never again spoke of it, at least in the mode of conversation, direct discussion, or even of correspondence. And these silences belong to that vertiginous abyss of the unsaid, above which is situated, I do not say is grounded, the memory of a friendship, as the renewed fidelity of a promise. This unsaid is not always what goes without saying, but it is also erased in the incessant movement of a writing that remains to be deciphered. For in a certain way, that of which Paul de Man says "perhaps we can speak of this again later" and of which I have just said we never again spoke, in truth, is what we have never ceased writing about ever since, as if to prepare ourselves to speak of it again one day, in our very old age. All in all, a promise. As if we had "given our word to each other." "To give each other the word," that is, to come to an agreement about the secret code of a rendez-vous, for example, and to "give his word," this is not exactly the same thing but are they dissociable? What is a "given word"? What is the meaning of a given word?

We should perhaps speak of this again some other time. I have already imposed upon your time enough. I now have to hurry to the conclusion and tell you, more summarily than ever, what I would have wished to elaborate at length if we had all the time we needed.

I would have wanted to speak to you of the thinking of Paul de Man and of "deconstruction in America" from the triple point of view of history, literature, and politics. A promise not kept but you will understand why I have used Rousseau to introduce these questions; I mean here the Rousseau of the *Social Contract* interpreted by Paul de Man. What de Man calls a "textual allegory" powerfully brings to light the "literarity" or "fictionality" of political discourse or rather of the promise written on the "politicity" of the political. And this structure of textual allegories which "generate history" is also presented, in a very precise sense of the term, as an "allegory of unreadability," that is to say, as an aporetic stucture: the madness of the promise and the madness of memory. The aporetic and madness. The word "aporia" recurs often in Paul de Man's last texts. I believe that we would misunderstand it if we tried to hold it to its most literal meaning: an absence of path, a paralysis before road-blocks, the immobilization of thinking, the impossibility of advancing, a barrier blocking the future. On the contrary, it seems to me that the experience of the aporia, such as de Man deciphers it, gives or promises the thinking of the path, provokes the thinking of the very possibility of what still remains unthinkable or unthought, indeed, impossible. The figures of rationality are profiled and outlined in the madness of the aporetic.

Now the aporetic always immobilizes us in the

simultaneously unsurpassable and unsatisfying system of an opposition, indeed, of a contradiction. The aporia is apparently, in its negative aspect, the negative contraction of the dialectic, a dialectic which does not find its path or its method, its grand methodical circle. A couple of examples used more than once by Paul de Man in order to describe this irreducible aporia: allegory *and* irony, the performative *and* the constative. It is above all in relation to the latter that the word "aporia" is indispensable to him. But each time, the aporia provokes a leap of memory and a displacement of thinking which leads us back not just toward an "older" unity than the opposition but also toward a new thinking of the disjunction, of a disjunction whose structure is wholly other, forgotten or yet to come, yet to come because forgotten, and always presupposed by the opposition. We have caught a glimpse of this through the couple allegory/irony in relation to "The Rhetoric of Temporality." It is clearer yet in the most recent texts in terms of the couple performative/constative. And aporicity evokes, rather than prohibits, more precisely, promises *through* its prohibition, an other thinking, an other text, the future of another promise. All at once the impasse (*the dead-end*) becomes the most "trustworthy," "reliable" place or moment for reopening a question which is finally equal to or on the same level as that which remains difficult to think. The rigorous demonstration of "Rhetoric of Persuasion (Nietzsche)" no doubt ends in an aporia, precisely in terms of the couple constative/performative, but this aporia evokes (*fait appel*), in some way situates, the place of evocation through an act of memory. This act calls us back to a time and place "before" oppositions (before the performative/constative opposition but also before that of literature and philosophy, and consequently many others); it therefore procures and promises a "somewhat more reliable point of 'reference' from which to ask the question." This "reliability" will no doubt be precarious and menaced by what renders all "promises" necessary and mad, but it will not promise itself any the less because of this. And what this *act* of memory promises is a thinking of the *act* which theorists of *speech acts* have never thought, not even suspected, even when they defined the performative as an *acting* word. After having analyzed the rhetorical structure of the "deconstruction of thought as act" in terms of Nietzsche (*AR*, p. 129), Paul de Man emphasizes fictionality and undecidability (another form of aporicity) in these terms:

The first passage (section 516) on identity showed that constative language is *in fact* [I again underline the singularity of this "in fact" in order to record it] performative, but the second passage (section 477) asserts that the possibility for language to perform is just as fictional as the possibility for language to assert. Since the analysis has been carried out on passages representative of Nietzsche's deconstructive procedure at its most advanced stage, it would follow that, in Nietzsche, the critique of metaphysics can be described as the deconstruction of the illusion that the language as truth (*episteme*) could be replaced by a language of persuasion (*doxa*). What seems to lead to an established priority of "setzen" over "erkennen," of language as action over language as truth, never quite reaches its mark. It under- or overshoots it and, in so doing, it reveals that the target which one long since assumed to have been eliminated has merely been displaced. The *episteme* has hardly been restored intact to its former glory, but it has not been definitively eliminated either. The differentiation between performative and constative language (which Nietzsche anticipates) is undecidable; the deconstruction leading from the one model to the other is irreversible but it always remains suspended, regardless of how often it is repeated.

Such an undecidability is the *condition* of all deconstruction: in the sense of condition of possibility, indeed, efficacy, and at the same time in the sense of situation or destiny. Deconstruction is, *on this condition* and *in this condition.* There is in this a power (a possibility) and a limit. But this limit, this finitude, empowers and makes one write; in a way it obliges deconstruction to write, to trace its path by linking its "act," always an act of memory, to the promised future of a text to be signed. The very oscillation of undecidability goes back and forth and weaves a text; it makes, if this is possible, a path of writing through the aporia. This is impossible, but no one has ever said that deconstruction, as a technique or a method, was possible; it thinks only on the level of the impossible and of what is still evoked as unthinkable. One of the interests of the passage that I have just quoted, as of the conclusion of "Promises (*Social Contract*)," consists of its rigorous determination of the textuality of the *text.* Paul de Man has just reached the point of giving a definition of rhetoric *as text* by passing by way of a thinking of deconstruction, that is to say, necessarily of an auto-deconstruction in which the *autos-* or the *self* would not be able to be either reflected or totalized, not even gathered or recollected, but only written and caught in the trap of the promise. Here is the said passage:

> Considered as persuasion, rhetoric is performative but when considered as a system of tropes, it deconstructs its own performance. Rhetoric is a *text* in that it allows for two incompatible, mutually self-destructive points of view, and therefore puts an insurmountable obstacle in the way of any reading or understanding. The aporia between performative

and constative language is merely a version of the aporia between trope and persuasion that both generates and paralyzes rhetoric and thus gives it the appearance of a history (*AR* p. 131).

It is thus necessary to think of rhetoric and history as this *text,* in terms of an aporia which, *because* it paralyzes, it also *engenders,* stimulates, makes one write, provokes thought, and confuses the limits between the realms of the text:

If the critique of metaphysics is structured as an aporia between performative and constative, this is the same as saying that it is structured as rhetoric. And since, if one wants to conserve the term "literature," one should not hesitate to assimilate it with rhetoric, then it would follow that the deconstruction of metaphysics, or "philosophy," is an impossibility to the precise extent that it is "literary." This by no means resolves the problem of the relation between literature and philosophy in Nietzsche, but it at least establishes a somewhat more reliable point of "reference" from which to ask the question (ibid.).

The formulation remains very prudent ("a somewhat more reliable. . ."; rather ironically, the word "reference" is in between quotation marks, and it is caught in the movement of a reading of Nietzsche). It is nonetheless a question of a strong recasting of what deconstruction can and could be, in its strategy and even in its politics.

One could demonstrate the continuity *and* the discontinuity of the de Manian project, after *Blindness and Insight,* especially in terms of the relations between deconstruction, rhetoric, literature, and history. In any case, the necessary transformation of the concept of the text makes inevitable the passage through textual events such as those whose memory and history we accumulate, for example, those accumulated under the name Rousseau or Nietzsche. They belong to the history or to the path of that singular aporia called "deconstruction."

There is no beyond-the-undecidable, but this beyond nevertheless remains to be thought from this "somewhat more reliable point of 'reference'"; and one can only be involved there in a promise, giving one's word on this subject, even if one denies it by signing ironically. There remains to be thought an other undecidability, one no longer bound to the order of *calculation* between two poles of opposition, but to the incalculable order of a wholly other: the coming or the call of the other. It must be unpredictable, aleatory beyond any caculation. *There is no* inside-the-undecidable, certainly, but an other memory calls us, recalls us to think an "act" or "*parole*" (speech), or a "speech act" which resists the opposition performative/constative, provoking at the same time the aporia and movement forward (*la marche*), the relation of one to the other, that is to say, history or the text. But we know, and we recalled it yesterday, that this singular memory *does not* lead us back to *any anteriority.* There never existed (there will never have existed) any older or more original "third term" that we would have to recall, toward which we would be called to recall *under* the aporetic disjunction. This is why what resists the non-dialectizable opposition, what "precedes" it in some way, will still bear the name of one of the terms and will maintain a *rhetorical* relation with the opposition. It will be figured, figurable. It will have the figure of opposition and will always let itself be parasited by it. We will call "act," for example, that act (of speech or not) which precedes the opposition between the language of act and the language of truth, between the performative and the constative. We could say the same thing for positing (*Setzung*, indeed, *Übersetzung*): even if it remains (as Heidegger says) a metaphysical determination of Being, it will give its name to a movement which cannot be reduced to metaphysics. The *staging* (*mise*) of the promise is a committed *positing* (*position*). We could say the same thing for words like "deconstruction" or "memory": memory without anteriority, memory of a past which has never been present, a memory without origin, a memory of the future, it is without an accepted or acceptable relation to what we commonly call "memory." We will, however, keep this name which can, under certain conditions of writing, allow something to which it appears unrelated to be thought. Whence the irreducibility of allegory, of rhetoric, and of that essential "unreadability" of the text: for example, of that movement whereby the deconstructive schema of a text *must* let itself be contaminated, parasited, by "relapsing" into the very thing that it deconstructs. Paul de Man calls this structure an "allegory of unreadability" (*AR*, p. 275). If this allegory is "metafigural," it is not in order to escape figurality, but, on the contrary, because it *remains* a figure of figure: "Such an allegory is meta-figural: it is an allegory of a figure (for example metaphor) which relapses into the figure it deconstructs. The *Social Contract* falls under this heading to the extent that it is indeed structured like an aporia: it persists in performing what it has shown to be impossible to do" (ibid.).

Rhetoric no longer designates only a constituted discipline, a system of techniques or discursive laws; it is always that, but it is also something else insofar as it at the same time writes, pledges and diverts a promise, a signature, a text: "Rhetoric is a text . . ."

Let us proceed quickly, still more quickly, and far too quickly. Let us situate three points, let us not say of a dispute, but of an *Auseinandersetzung* between deconstruction and a certain voice of the Heideggerian text (less than ever I would say here all the voices and the entire text of Heidegger). But the voice in question often appears dominant.

1. In the same way that he says "science does not think," or "the essence of technology is nothing technological," Heidegger would say, within the same "logic": rhetoric is only a determined discipline or area, a belated and even "technological one," it concerns only a modality of speech; thinking speech, the thinking of rhetoricity itself is not rhetorical; he has said the same thing about linguistics or semiotics. Now in this, at least, deconstruction is no longer "Heideggerian": yes, science can think, the essence of technology and the thinking of this essence retain *something* technological, and the thinking of rhetoricity is neither above it, nor before it, nor elsewhere; it is not foreign to rhetoric. It is precisely this hierarchy, this limit, this purity, reclaimed by Heidegger, that is *deconstructed*, that deconstructs itself, that "deconstructs," as Paul de Man says in another context, "the very notion of the self" (*AR*, p. 173). From then on, each deconstructive thinking constitutes a text which bears its rhetorical singularity, the figure of its signature, its pathos, its apparatus, its style of promise, etc. Heidegger's text is *also* a rhetoric—a textual rhetoric—and we must be able to analyze it as such. There is no "deconstruction in America" without *this* relation to Heidegger. In terms of the thousands of ways imaginable, one can certainly not circumvent the necessity of all the Heideggerian trajectories, one cannot be any "nearer" to this thinking, but one cannot also not be any farther from it, nor can one be any more hetero-

geneous (this does not mean opposed) to it than by
risking an affirmation of this type: the essence of this is
this, the essence of technology is (still) technological,
there is no gap or abyss between thinking thought or
thinking memory (*Gedächtnis*) and science, technology,
writing (mnemonics); or rather, this maintainance, in a
Heideggerian manner, of a heterogeneity between the
essence of technology and technology (which is, by the
way, one of the most traditional of gestures), between
thinking memory and science, thinking memory and
technicist writing, is precisely a protection against an
other abyssal risk, that of parasitic contamination, of an
an-oppositional différance, etc. We cannot exaggerate
the risk and the gravity of this brief sentence (for example): the essence of technology is not foreign to technology. Apparently very trivial, it can yet again put into
question, with all of the entailing consequences, the
scope of even the most fundamental philosophical
gesture.

    2. Can memory without anteriority, that is to
say, without origin, become a Heideggerian theme? I do
not believe so. With all the precautions that must be
taken here, we cannot erase from the Heideggerian text
an indispensable reference to originarity, even if we do
not grant the latter any etymological status. We could
give numerous examples of this; let us content ourselves
with the following since it concerns memory: "The originary word (*das anfängliche Wort*) 'Gedanc' means: the
gathered, all-gathering recollection (*das gesammelte,
alles versammelnde Gedenken*). 'The Gedanc' says nearly the
same thing as 'the soul' (*das Gemüt*), 'spirit' (*der muot*),
'the heart' (*das Herz*). Thinking, in the sense of this originally speaking word (*im Sinne des anfänglich sagenden
Wortes*)' Gedanc,' is almost more original (*ursprünglicher*)

than that thinking of the heart which Pascal, centuries later and already as a countermove against mathematical thinking, attempted to recover." (. . .) "The original Being of memory rules (*waltet das ursprüngliche Wesen des Gedächtnisses*) in the originary word 'Gedanc' (*im anfänglichen Wort der 'Gedanc'*)" (Eng. pp. 139 and 141; Ger. pp. 91 and 93). By making the auto-deconstruction of the Hegelian "cornerstone" manifest, de Man again puts into question that originarism which would situate thinking memory outside of and sheltered from technology, science, and writing. Memory which thinks in terms of oppositions, even those which are dialectical, of allegory and irony, the performative and the constative, etc., does not lay bare any more secret origin. It continues to write and promises the rhetoric of another text.

3. Above all, it does not think itself as gathering; it never reduces the disjunctive difference. We have insisted enough upon the de Manian motif of *disjunction*; I will not return to it. On the other hand, how can we deny that, for Heidegger, the essence of memory resides primarily, originally, in gathering (*Versammlung*), even if we distinguish it from any synthesis, syntax, or composition? Here are some examples—already cited—among many others: "Initially (*anfänglich*), 'memory' (*Gedächtnis*) did not at all mean the power to recall (*Erinnerungsvermögen*). The word designates the whole *soul* in the sense of a constant, *interior* gathering (*innigen Versammlung*, I underline "soul" and "interior") . . . " Further on: "We have determined Memory as the gathering of devoted thinking (*Versammlung des Andenkens*)" (Eng. 140 and 150; Ger. 92 and 97). The degradation of this original meaning, its "wasting away," its "shrinking" and its "impoverishment" are attributed to

scholastic philosophy, as well as to "techno-scientific" definitions.

This interpretation—and this rhetoric—also determine a politics: not only in regard to history, to technology and science, but also in regard to rhetoric and politics, to writing and literary writing. We saw yesterday how Heidegger would have determined their appurtenance, outside of, at the "exit" of, and sheltered from thinking or poetry. It is at this point, if we had enough time, that I would have liked to speak to you of the politics of "deconstruction in America," in particular, of de Manian deconstruction. It cannot be deciphered, it seems to me, except in terms of the proximity and divergence whose enigma we have just perceived. Both inside and outside of academic institutions. Every reading proposed by Paul de Man, and recently rendered more and more explicitly, says something about institutional structures and the political stakes of hermeneutic conflicts. The characteristics of these readings are most often discreet, but always clear and incisive, and always directed not so much against the profession or the institution, but against the academisms of the right and the left, against the conservatism that apolitical traditionalists and activists share in common. The introduction to "Hegel on the Sublime"[9] describes these "symmetrical gestures." "Reactionaries" and "political activists" in truth misunderstand, in order to protect themselves, the political stake and structure of the text, the political allegory of the literary text, no less than the allegorical and literary structure of the political text. More and more Paul de Man publicly took part in the politico-institutional debates surrounding deconstruction. The positions he took do not have the coded simplicity of well known oppositions, of predictable and unpardonably tiresome predications. Paul de Man's "politics" cannot be separated, neither in its acts nor in what it leaves to be deciphered, from that thinking of the political and of the law which traverses all of his writings. Here again the reading of Rousseau, no less than that of Nietzsche, should be followed as one would follow a red thread. The word "political" is perhaps no longer only appropriate; it is also allegorical. *Political Allegory* was the first title of *Promises* and that essay begins by demonstrating the impossibility of rescuing the "referential status" of terms like "political," "religious," "ethical," "theoretical," etc. Each of these "thematic categories" "is torn apart by the aporia that constitutes it." But what this same text (for example) signs, announces, *promises* on the subject of law, the act and the promise, forms the best introduction, it seems to me, to what could be considered Paul de Man's relation to the "political," to what we tranquilly and commonly call politics, to his "experience" of the thing. Let us go further and, for want of time, even more quickly: the "definition" of the text which is formulated in *Promises* in an explicit and insistent fashion, even while leaving the word "definition" between quotation marks ["We call *text* any entity that. . . . The 'definition' of the text. . . ." (p. 270) announced by a "We have moved closer and closer to the 'definition' of *text* (p. 268)], has a privileged relation to the political. The legal or political text makes more explicit and better reveals the very structure of the text in general. It "defines" it better than any other ext. And there is no "politics" without this text. To distort things in another way, as false as the inverse, certain people would say that there is nothing apolitical in deconstruction, but rather an excessive "politicism." Paul de Man writes, for example: "The structure of the entity with which we are concerned (be it as property, as national State or any other political insitution) is *most clearly revealed* when it is considered as the general form that subsumes all these particular versions, namely as legal *text*" (p. 267, de Man emphasizes the word "text," I emphasize the others). From this point of view, there is no contradiction between "revolution and legality": the text of law is, "per definition, in a condition of unpredictable change. Its mode of existence is necessarily temporal and historical, though in a strictly non-teleological sense" (pp. 266-67). Such a sentence makes precise a certain strategy of Paul de Man's most recent texts in terms of historicity: it is "defined" in terms of a new "definition" of the *text,* and it diverges from the dominant philosophical, that is to say, teleological, concept of history. We know that this concept still largely dominates the most "modern" political discourses (whether or not they pass themselves off as revolutionary). Further on, he writes:

> There can be no text without grammar: the logic of grammar generates texts only in the absence of referential meaning, but every text *generates* a referent that *subverts* the grammatical principle to which it owed its constitution. What remains hidden in the everyday use of language, the fundamental incompatibility between grammar and meaning, *becomes explicit when the linguistic structures are stated, as is the case here, in political terms. (AR* p. 269)

I also emphasize the word "generates" in order to draw attention to a perhaps less apparent but no less essential dimension of deconstruction, whether it is a question of effects of reference or effects of history. This same essay ends, we remember, with these words: " . . . textual allegories . . . *generate* history"].

There is no politics without "action" or without

an "active" text. And we rediscover here the same injunction: memory or promise, memory as promise of an *act* which, in order not to belong to the opposition act/non-act, action/theory, performative/constative, is nevertheless not *anterior* to them, neither in the mode of past anterior nor in the mode of future anterior. It is again the *definition of the text* which says this act beyond the act. I have already quoted a part of this passage, let us quote a little more:

> A text is defined by the necessity of considering a statement, *at the same time* [and it is the time of this *same time* which evokes an other thinking of what is found in action here] as performative and constative, and the logical tension between figure and grammar is repeated in the impossibility of distinguishing between two linguistic functions which are not necessarily compatible. It seems that as soon as a text knows what it states, it can only *act* deceptively, like the thieving lawmaker in the *Social Contract,* and if a text does not *act,* it cannot state what it knows. The distinction between a text as narrative and a text as theory also belongs to this field of tension. (*AR,* p. 270, my emphasis)

This *same time* never is, will never have been and will never be *present.* De Man speaks later on of that "absence of an *état présent*" in the Rousseauistic aporia of the promise and in the legislator's imposture. There is only the promise and memory, memory as promise, without any gathering possible in the form of the present. This disjunction is the law, the text of law and the law of the text. The promise prohibits the gathering of Being in presence, being even its condition. The condition of the possibility and impossibility of eschatology, the ironic allegory of messianism.[10]

From the beginning of this trajectory, in terms of the debate surrounding Hölderlin concerning the law and the gathering of Being, we have never been further from Heidegger. And, yet, Paul de Man himself says, an opposition never excludes, on the contrary, the most troubling affinities. For Heidegger's thinking *is not simply* a thinking of gathering. The end of *Was heisst Denken?*, for example, where we have followed the trace of memory (*Gedächtnis*) as originary gathering (*Versammlung*), also opens on to the *khorismos* of the *khora,* to the disjunction of the place (*Ort*), to the topical difference (*Verschiendenheit der Ortung*) between being (present) and Being, to duplicity (*Zwiefalt*), difference (*Unterschied*), etc. No doubt, thinking memory (*Gedächtnis*) is itself the gathering of this difference, and it could be the same for all disjunction as such. But this gathering does not gather in an "état présent." It does not even gather Being, it *calls* and *gives* us to thinking (*donne à penser*). Having reached this point and still much too schematically, it would be necessary to recall that for Heidegger, too, memory is, like the promise, and, again in the words of Paul de Man, "future oriented and prospective": memory also gathers near what "can come" (Eng. 140; Ger. 92), it also tends toward the "future" (ibid.). It thinks only by *giving* what is to be thought or in thinking what calls and *gives* to be thought. *Was heisst Denken?* is not only a meditation on memory, it is also, with the same step (*pas*), in the same march, that singular overflow of the question of Being by the question of the gift (of the *Gabe* of the *es gibt Sein*). "What calls us to think, gives us over to thinking" (*Was uns denken heisst, gibt uns zu denken*). And later, as in *Zeit und Sein,* the meditation on this gift (*Gabe*), gift of Being and gift of time, unfolds the question of Being and the calling of Being *as* the question of the gift. There is Being, but this "*es gibt*" never gives anything that is a "present" or that is gathered in a present; it calls as a promise, it calls itself a promise, a commitment, an invitation. Heidegger names the promise in the same movement and at bottom we have never been nearer to Paul de Man's "*Die Sprache verspricht (sich)*." Heidegger never signed it, but who signs a promise? He wrote the following which speaks of the meaning of a given word:

> "To call" (*Heissen*), in short, means "to command," presupposing that we hear this word, too, in its original sense. For, at bottom, "to command" means not: to give a command or an order, but: to commend, to entrust, to give over to the protection of, to keep safely (*einer Geborgenheit anheimgeven, bergen*). To call is to call out in the form of a commendation, to call into arrival by referring. . . . A promise (*Verheissung*) signifies: a word which calls and assures in such a way that what is said here is a commitment, a given "word" (*ein Versprochenes*). [The French translator uses the word "parole," which he places between quotation marks, to translate "*ein Versprochenes*": a given word, what is promised in a promise.] (Eng. 118; Ger. 83)

No path is possible without the aporia of the gift, which does not occur without the aporia of the promise. I have tried to show elsewhere, in a seminar on the gift (given at Yale on Paul de Man's invitation), that there is no gift except on the aporetic condition that nothing is given that is *present* and that *presents* itself as such. The gift is only a promise and a promised memory, here the future of Mnemosyne, I mean the future of the *Mnemosyne* of Hölderlin, of Heidegger, of Paul de Man in America. For after having recalled the gift and then responded to the question of this gift (*Gabe*), to the question of what gives us the most to think about: "What gives us the most to think about in our thinking time is that we do not yet think," Heidegger then quotes "Mnemosyne":

When man is being drawn (*auf dem Zug*) towards what withdraws (*in das Sichentziehende*), he indicates (*Zeigt*) what withdraws. In this movement we are a sign (*Auf dem Zug dahin sind wir ein Zeichen*). But what we indicate in this way is something that is not translated (*übersetzt*), not yet translated, into the language we speak (*in die Sprache unseres Sprechens*). It remains without signification (*Es bleibt ohne Deutung*). We are an unreadable sign (*ein deutungslose Zeichen*).

In his draft for the hymn entitled "Mnemosyne" (*Gedächtnis*), Hölderlin says:

> We are a sign, unreadable,
> *Ein Zeichen sind wir, deutungslos,*
> We are without pain, and we have
> *Schmerzlos sind wir, und haben fast*
> Almost lost language in a foreign place.
> *Die Sprache in der Fremde Verloren.*
>
> (Eng. 18; Ger. 6)

To lose one's language in a foreign place, this was certainly not a fate reserved for deconstruction in America, nor the destination reserved only for Hölderlin, Heidegger, or Paul de Man outside of their native languages. This experience, let us risk saying this perhaps against Heidegger's intention, is the terrible chance of the promise, of the given word in the *sich Versprechen* of the *Sprache*.

I no longer know what I promised, nor to whom, in coming here, to the far West of America, to speak to you on memory in memory, in this memory where I shall always be, in this memory of Paul de Man.

It is always necessary to excuse oneself for appropriating to oneself this work of mourning. It is always

necessary to excuse oneself for giving, for a gift must
never appear in a present, given the risk of its being
annulled in thanks, in the symbolic, in exchange or
economy, indeed, of its becoming a benefit. It is necessary to be forgiven for appearing to give. But if there is
no gift, only the promise, it is also always necessary to
excuse oneself for promising. For a promise is neither
possible nor tenable. We have not read the last chapter
of *Allegories of Reading*. Like all of Paul de Man's work, it
still awaits us, in advance of us. The next-to-last chapter
is entitled "Promises (*Social Contract*)," the last, "Excuses
(*Confessions*)."

What is love, friendship, memory, from the moment two impossible promises are involved with them,
sublimely, without any possible exchange, in difference and dysymmetry, in the incommensurable? What
are we, who are we, to what and to whom *are we*, and
to what and to whom are we *destined* in the experience of this impossible promise? Henceforth: what is
experience?

These questions can be posed only after the death
of a friend, and they are not limited to the question of
mourning. What should we think of all of this, of love,
of memory, of promise, of destination, of experience,
since a promise, from the first moment that it pledges,
and however possible it appears, pledges beyond death,
beyond what we call, without knowing of what or of
whom we speak, death. It involves, in reverse, the other,
dead *in us*, from the first moment, even if no one is *there*
to respond to the promise or speak for the promise.
What does "*in us*" mean if such an impossible promise
is *thinkable*, that is to say, possible in its impossibility?
This is, perhaps, what thinking gives us to think about,
what gives us to think about thinking.

A promise cannot be kept, it cannot even be made in all its purity. As if it were always linked to the departed other, as if it were therefore not linked. But consequently, this is because a promise pledges only to what is mortal. A promise has meaning and gravity only on the condition of death, when the living person is one day all alone with his promise. A promise has meaning and gravity only with the death of the other. When the friend is no longer *there*, the promise is still not tenable, it will not have been made, but as a trace of the future it can still be *renewed*. You could call this an act of memory or a given word, even an act of faith; I prefer to take the risk of a singular and more equivocal word. I prefer to call this an *act*, only an act, quite simply an act. An impossible act, therefore the only one worthy of its name, or rather which, in order to be worthy of its name, must be worthy of the name of the other, made in the name of the other. Try and translate, in all of its syntactical equivocity, a syntagm such as "donner au nom d l'autre" or "une parole donnée au nom d l'autre." In a single sentence, it could mean in French, or rather in English: "to give to the name of the other" and "to give in the name of the other." Who knows what we are doing when we donnons au nom de l'autre?

Notes

1. *What is Called Thinking?*, trans. by Glenn Gray (New York: Harper and Row, 1968), pp. 138-39, 144. [Translator's note: in almost all cases I have retranslated the passages cited from this translation in order to have them conform more closely to the German. For the German see Martin Heidegger, *Was heisst Denken?* (Tübingen: Max Niemeyer Verlag, 1954), pp. 91 and 57. Subsequent references to this text will be to page numbers in these editions and will be cited parenthetically within the body of the essay by "Eng." and "Ger.," respectively.]

2. *Allegories of Reading: Figural Language in Rousseau, Nietzsche, Rilke, and Proust* (New Haven: Yale University Press, 1979), p. 277. [TN: Further references to this text will be inserted parenthetically in the essay by *AR* and page number.]

3. Rousseau, *Correspondance générale* (Paris: Librairie Armand Colin, 1924), 12: 110.

4. Here is one example, among many others, of such an evaluation (it would be necessary to devote more than a note to it); I cite it here because it belongs to the same context:

. . . these poems are not properly literature. Literature is literally that which is written down and rewritten, and whose destination is to be accessible to the public for reading (*einer Öffentlichkeit für das Lesen*). In this way, literature becomes the object of widely diverging interests which, in their turn, are once again stimulated in a literary way—through criticism and publicity. That an individual may find his way out of the literary industry and find his way thoughtfully and even edifyingly to poesy is never enough to render to poesy (*Dichtung*) its essential place (*Wesensort*). . . .

Occidental poesy and European literature are two abysmally different, essential forces in our history. We probably still have only an entirely inadequate notion of the being and significance of the literary phenomena.

However, through the literary, as their common medium, poesy and thought and science are mutually assimilated to one another (*Durch das Literarische und in ihm als ihrem Medium sind nun aber Dichten und Denken und Wissenschaft einander angeglichen*). When thinking is set off from science (*sich gegen die Wissenschaft absetzt*), it appears, from the point of view of science, as a failed poeticizing. When, on the other hand, thinking knowingly escapes from the proximity of poesy, it likes to appear as the super-science which would surpass all sciences in scientificity.

Still, precisely because thinking is not poetry, but an originary saying and speaking of language (*ursprungliches Sagen und Sprechen der Sprache*), it must remain in proximity to poesy. But because science does not think, thinking must, in its current situation, insistently watch over the sciences, which is what they cannot do for themselves. . . .

. . . The essential relation is determined rather by a fundamental trait of the modern era, to which the literary phenomena mentioned above also belongs. It can be briefly characterized as follows: that which is appears today primarily in *that* object-materiality which, through the scientific-objectification of all regions and domains, is installed and maintained under domination. . . .

We do not notice *the scientifico-literary objectification* (*die wissenschaftlich literarische Vergegenständlichung*) of that which is, because we move within it (Eng. 134-5; Ger. 154).

I have chosen this passage and I have emphasized these words in it because they concern a sort of *negative privilege* of literature in the objectivist confusion denounced by Heidegger. It is the medium, the element of confusion, between science, poesy, and thinking, and it requires a scientificoliterary objectivation.

The division, evaluation, and subordination are incontestable. And they concern writing in general as well as literary writing. They *come out* of thinking, they leave it, and do so in order to fall, in order to protect themselves from it. While reserving the right to return to the following passage at another time, I shall here simply refer to it and cite it: "Socrates, throughout his life and right up to his death, did nothing else than place himself and maintain himself in the draft of this current. This is why he is the purest thinker of the West. This is why he wrote nothing. For he who begins to write on coming out of thought (*aus dem Denken*) will inevitably resemble those people who run to seek refuge against a strong draft. This remains the secret of an as yet hidden history: that all Western thinkers after Socrates, notwithstanding their greatness, had to be such "fugitives" [Heidegger does not, himself, place quotations around "Flüchtlinge"]. Thinking has entered into literature. And literature has decided the fate of Western science, which, by way of the *doctrina* of the Middle Ages, became the *scientia* of modernity. In this form, all sciences have sprung, in a double manner, from out of philosophy. The sciences come here out of philosophy in that they must leave it" (Eng. 17-8; Ger. 52).

5. Austin, *Philosophical Papers*, ed. by J. O. Urmson and G. J. Warnock (Oxford: Clarendon Press, 1979), pp. 55-75. [TN: Further references to this essay will be cited parenthetically within the text by *PP* and page number.]

6. *Blindness and Insight: Essays in the Rhetoric of Contemporary Criticism* (Minneapolis: University of Minnesota Press, 1983), p. xii. [TN: Hereafter cited within the text by *BI* and page number.]

7. On the interpretation of this sentence, see Rodolphe Gasché's "Deconstruction as Criticism" in *Glyph 6* (Baltimore: The Johns Hopkins University Press, 1979) and his "'Setzung' and 'Übersetzung': Notes on Paul de Man" in *Diacritics,* (Winter 1981) vol. 11, no. 4, and Suzanne Gearhart's "Philosophy *Before* Literature: Deconstruction, Historicity, and the Work of Paul de Man" in *Diacritics* (Winter 1983) vol. 13, no. 4; but also Richard Klein's "The Blindness of Hyperboles, the Ellipses of Insight" in *Diacritics* (Summer 1973) as well as David Carroll's "Representation or the End(s) of History, Dialectics and Fiction" [in *Yale French Studies* (1980), 59:220] and *The Subject in Question: The Languages of Theory and the Strategies of Fiction* [(Chicago: University of Chicago Press, 1982), especially pages 197ff and 212], a book which debates with Paul de Man on other themes, especially around the reading of Lukács.

8. I ought to cite here a passage from De Man's early text, "The Rhetoric of Temporality": "Irony is unrelieved *vertige*, dizziness to the point of madness [we could play here on the French word "vertige": as we say in French, it makes one's head turn, and it is the experience of a turn—that is, of a trope which cannot stop turning and turning around, since we can only speak of a (rhetorical) turn by way of another trope, without any chance of achieving the stability of a metalanguage, a metatrope, a metarhetoric: the

irony of irony of which Schlegel speaks and which De Man cites is still an irony: whence the madness of the regressus ad infinitum, and the madness of rhetoric, whether it be that of irony or that of allegory: madness because it has no reason to stop, because reason is tropic]. Sanity can exist only because we are willing to function within the conventions of duplicity and dissimulation, just as social language dissimulates the inherent violence of the actual relationship between human beings." And elsewhere in the same text: ". . . absolute irony is a consciousness of madness, itself the end of all consciousness; it is a consciousness of a non-consciousness, a reflection on madness from the inside of madness itself. But this reflection is made possible only by the double structure of ironic language" (*BI*, pp. 215-6). This, it seems to me, is another way of protecting the concept of irony from its German-Romantic determination, from what probably Schlegel and certainly Hegel ascribe to it; namely, a movement or structure of that mastering consciousness which rises above finite determinations.

9. "Hegel on the Sublime" in M. Krupnick, ed., *Displacement* (Bloomington: Indiana University Press, 1983).

10. These lectures were written when Thomas Pepper gave me a copy of a text by Peter Szondi: "Hope in the Past: On Walter Benjamin" [translated and published in *Critical Inquiry* (Spring 1978), vol. 4]. I cite it here, because of its allusions to the messianism of all promises, but also because, aside from its *Auseinandersetzung* with Benjamin, Paul de Man argues with Szondi in "Sign and Symbol in Hegel's *Aesthetics* [In *Critical Inquiry* (Summer 1982), vol. 8]. I will cite, in English, only a few lines from this reading of Benjamin (and of Proust): "In the theses on the concept of history that Benjamin wrote shortly before his death, we again find the statement from the *One-Way Street* that 'memory points out to every one in the book of life writing which, invisibly, glossed the text as prophecy.' But this is embedded in a philosophy of history. 'The past,' writes Benjamin here, 'carries with it a temporal idea, according to which it is assigned to salvation' " (503).